PRAISE FOR SCOTT GUERIN

"The author's careful illustration of his introduction to religion, description of his devout faith that was punctuated by nagging questions, his approach to seeking the answers, and his interpretation of his findings are a refreshing account of a journey that offers numerous perspectives along the way. **A highly recommended read that demonstrates how curiosity and the questioning of traditional thinking can illuminate many different paths** to exploring an individual's spiritual journey."
— Jill Cantelmo, PhD

"If you have ever pondered the seemingly endless questions about God, religion, or spirituality, this book will get you thinking. **The author examines myriad religious/spiritual uncertainties and conundrums**, inevitably ones you have wrestled with yourself."
— Mark Vogel, PsyD

"Life is a journey, and **you come away from reading this book feeling confident** in all its twists and turns. Anyone who questions their faith, or struggles to accept the religious beliefs of their parents will find comfort in this intimate story."
— Maureen Saks

"The author takes us along his own heartfelt journey and explains how he became open and enlightened spiritually. **He also uses a more scientific approach to back up his spiritual beliefs**. I would highly recommend this book to anyone who struggles with the rigidity and exclusive nature of traditional religions."
— Amazon Reviewer

"I thoroughly enjoyed Dr. Guerin's account of his journey, starting from his boyhood Lutheran upbringing, through an evangelical Christian phase as a teenager and young adult, to a more spiritual approach as an older adult. The account effectively weaves the author's scholarly research into an easy-to-read and interesting personal narrative. **I finished the book anxious to learn more.**"
— Amazon Reviewer

ANGEL
IN TRAINING

A Spiritual Journey

2nd Ed.

SCOTT GUERIN PH.D.

For more information, visit Angelintraining.org

Copyright ©2020 Scott A. Guerin

ISBN: 978-0-578-72722-6

Second Edition

Cover design and logo developed by Jeremy Mayes
jeremy@amayes.me

Printed and bound in Canada.

The author greatly appreciates you taking the time to read this work. Please consider leaving a review wherever you bought the book, or telling your friends or blog readers about *Angel In Training* to help spread the word. Thank you for your support.

Angel In Training. Copyright © 2020 by Scott A. Guerin. All rights reserved under International and Pan-American Copyright Conventions. This book is sold subject to the condition that it shall not, by way of trade or otherwise, be lent, re-sold, hired out, or otherwise circulated without the publisher's prior consent in any form of binding or cover other than that in which it is published and without a similar condition including this condition being imposed on the subsequent purchaser.

CONTENTS

Praise for Scott Guerin 1
Acknowledgments 9
Angels 11

PART 1:
Learning about God, Religion, and Life 13

The Spark 14
God—Take one 21
The Good, the Bad, and the Family 26
Dad, a Correlate of God 32
If It's Not One Thing, It's Your Mother 37
There's Got to Be Something Else 41
Enter Sin 44
God and Family 46
Wing and a Prayer 50
Getting Serious 53
Born Again 56
The "Non" Denomination 60
The Flame 67
The Aftermath 71
Slow Deliberation 73
Cornered! 77
Looking for That Born Again Feeling 84
Swing and a Miss 89
Prayer from a Different Place 99
The in Crowd 104
X Goes to Seminary 110
Confrontation 111

Beginning of the Devil 116
Possession Part 1 120
Possession Part 2 125
Push Back 129
Implosion of X 136
One Step to the Left 144
Slow Burn 149
Decompensation 151
Rock Bottom 155

PART TWO
Moving Beyond Religion 163

Looking into the Abyss 164
Commonly Confused Topics 168
What, Wait ... There Are Others? 174
Contrary to ... your Own Beliefs 186
How Do We Know Anything? 191
Prayer—The Sequel 196
Praying for Others—The Results 200
Meditation—A Common Ground 206
The Game Changer—A Conversation with God 212
The Next Course—Miracles 226
A Word about Automatic Writing 229
Angel, Realized 236
Prayer 2.0—Attraction 239
How the Law of Attraction Works 245
A Quantum Explanation 262
On Being Angels 270

12 Lessons 274
Suggested Readings 276
References 278

To Debbie,
my only passenger on this wild ride.
Your love was a rock during the challenging times,
love you bb.

OTHER BOOKS BY SCOTT GUERIN

Other books in the Angel in Training Series by Scott Guerin

Angel in Training
12 Lessons: A Path Forward
Calling All Angels!

ACKNOWLEDGMENTS

On our journey through this life, the most powerful lessons learned often occur as a result of our relationships with others. In these pages, I recount many discussions, laughs, arguments, and heart-wrenching stories involving dozens of people. These interactions were critical in my development and the evolving understanding of God, myself, and spirituality. I thank you all and am deeply grateful for those that cared enough to work with me. Some of you know who you are, others I have not been in contact with for many years. In either case, all names have been changed to ensure privacy.

Families are the crucible of life. Growing up with our parents and siblings is where we are pressure-tested as we become the people we want to be. Our family also provides a first take on the world. Much of our initial perspectives about God, religion, and spirituality are developed at home, interacting with parents, siblings, and in the religion in which we were raised. My family was no different. I've shared most aspects of this book with them along the way, well almost all of them. I love my parents, sister, and brother deeply and know I was loved from day one.

No one has helped me more to bring this book to fruition than my wife Debbie. She knows most of the characters well, and me the most. She also read and reread the manuscript many times, offering the most valuable comments a writer can receive; "This part is too long." or, "This chapter is very good." or, "This sentence doesn't make sense."

I would not have completed this book without the support of my friend and author, Dr. Mark Vogel. I am honored to have gained invaluable insights from his razor-sharp mind in addition to his ongoing encouragement to put my story to paper. Also, special thanks to Jennifer Walkup, who's editorial skills helped me bring the many milestone events and stories to life.

I want to emphasize an important point here. In this book, I have attempted to convey my spiritual journey, as you will see, it has taken many twists and turns. My greatest hope is that some aspects of my experiences can help others as they traverse their journey through this life. My point is, if you are happy with your current beliefs, religion, or practices, *please* do not make any changes. Your life is all about you and your happiness.

ANGELS

In many religions, angels are considered spiritual beings, agents, or messengers of God. The word comes from the Greek *agnelos*, meaning messenger. In Islam, belief in angels is one of the Six Articles of Faith. Devas and dharma protectors are types of angelic beings in Buddhism and Hinduism. Other religions believe each person has a guardian angel to help them throughout life. The Judeo-Christian Bible provides detailed descriptions of angels with different powers and abilities. Interestingly, when angels are mentioned in these scriptures, they usually appear in human form.

One day, I realized we are all angels.

PART 1
LEARNING ABOUT GOD, RELIGION, AND LIFE

THE SPARK

"Well, Scott," the pastor said, then paused. A wave of surprise washed over his face. After a long moment, he placed his hand on my shoulder, leaned close to me, and whispered, "I'm sorry." Looking down sheepishly, he added, "It's a tough job."

Then silence.

He and I were standing in the narthex of our Lutheran Church after the second morning service, as dozens of people departed the sanctuary. Sunlight streamed in the numerous tall windows in the sanctuary, flooding the adjacent narthex through glass doors and panels. The upbeat hymn the organist played was almost drowned out by parishioners talking and greeting each other with hugs, kisses, and big smiles. Children skipped and ran around, many toward the exit to freedom. The boys tugged at their ties and tight-fitting collars.

Only a few minutes before, the service concluded, and the pastor passed me as he left the sanctuary and headed to his office to change out of his robes. He was a tall man with a round face and short, dark, thinning hair. The patches of gray on the sides and sideburns enhanced his already authoritative features. He always appeared larger-than-life to me as he seemed to glide by in his floor-length white robe to his office as if he was a divine superhero returning to his lair. That day, I had waited for him to emerge, as usual, in his nicely fitted three-piece suit and tie.

I had waited for weeks to ask him a few questions, and although I still felt reluctant to approach him, I had finally mustered up enough nerve to go for it that day. I even had an ice-breaker question ready to get the conversation started: the real, and far more important question, related to my thoughts of leaving the Lutheran church.

My ice breaker concerned the pastor's Sunday sermons. Because I was such a nerd, I began taking notes on his sermons in seventh grade. This was a year ahead of the requirement to hand in sermon notes in order to be confirmed as a Lutheran. When I began my official note-taking the following year in eighth grade, I noticed he repeated sermons from the year before. This surprised and puzzled me because the pastor's role in the church, in my perspective, was to teach us to about God and inform us of what God wanted us to learn. The Sunday sermons were the best way to convey what God was thinking. Trying to rationalize the repeated sermons, I gave him the benefit of the doubt and figured there was some divinely inspired reason. Maybe we were not learning what God wanted to teach us during that particular week. Perhaps God directed him to repeat sermons because we needed to hear them again. I was sure there was some explanation of why God led him to preach these sermons again. So, once he addressed that question, I could continue with my other concern about the church.

ANGEL IN TRAINING

To my surprise, his response dashed all hopes of any real explanation about why he recycled his sermons. That's it? "It's a tough job?" Nothing else? No advice, no reassuring words of wisdom? There had to be something more profound, more in-depth, farther reaching. Anything, please! Yet, his words were clear. It was like when the curtain is pulled from the control booth in *The Wizard of Oz*, revealing a bumbling man working shifts and levers to operate the Great and Powerful Oz. Was the pastor a similar fake? What would he do now that I knew? Would he tell my parents? What could I do?

At that moment, he must have known his response had an impact on me. I'm sure my expression and body language were telegraphing my dismay. He straightened his posture, and his pastoral appearance returned. Just then, a parishioner walked up to us. The pastor quickly turned to them and said, "Scott and I were just finishing up. See you next week, Scott," and began a conversation with them.

Other kids my age may not have thought it was a big deal. So what? Maybe he was busy with other things, or preaching was not his strength. But I was not other kids. I was in an emotional and existential crisis. I was counting on this person, this man of God, to help me work through this turmoil to solid ground.

Dismayed and profoundly deflated, I politely said I would see him next week and walked away in a daze.

That was the moment my journey began. The effect the conversation had on me was not just because of my pastor's equivocal answer and reaction, but because it came at a crucial time in my life. Looking back, I can see how I was primed for this event. My personality, combined with my age, and home life in a family of intense individuals, were all factors that made this exchange powerful and memorable. The momentum of this event propelled me for decades on a spiritual journey that took me to unexpected places. My search for answers led me through organized religion, other spiritual sources, and the disciplines of psychology and quantum physics.

This brief but poignant conversation took place in the winter of 1972. I was fourteen and in the eighth grade. We were members of the Redeemer Lutheran Church in New Jersey and the reason we attended this church, as far as I knew, was because my mother's parents were both born in Finland and their Norwegian heritage included the Lutheran faith. My parents didn't know much about religion, or at least I didn't think they did because they didn't talk about it much. My mom was more motivated in attending than my dad, but I don't remember him complaining. Mom took the lead in organizing the family every Sunday morning, starting with breakfast, pushing us to keep moving, get dressed in our Sunday clothes, and piling us into the car. Mom and Dad both were in the choir, and I think they went to adult Sunday school classes sometimes. This environment was where I initially learned about God, why we had to go to church, and what we had to do to go to heaven. Being my first experience, I have many special memories of this church.

The lobby or narthex of the building followed traditional Lutheran design and architecture. I felt at home going there, but always with some concern because God was supposed to be there too. The building was situated on the corner of two well-traveled roads, with a large parking lot and areas of grass in the front and far side of the building. It was a picture-perfect postcard of a suburban church.

The only access to the church was via a sprawling parking lot. For many years, it was a gravel lot, and I still remember the crunching and popping noise the stones made as car after car entered the lot. Now and then, we could hear a loud pop and a clink when a stone powerfully launched against another car's hub cap or siding. We had the most fun walking on the logs that served as a boundary between the parking lot and grass. They were six or eight-foot sections of telephone poles lying from a few inches to a few feet apart end to end of three sides of the lot. We pretended that the logs were floating in hot lava and falling off the log was instant death. Unless, of course, someone had asbestos shoes which protected you against the 2,100-degree heat for five seconds on the rare occasion they fell into the lava. One could also be protected by asbestos clothing that offered the same safeguard, unless, someone "called" no asbestos clothing allowed. Well, then you were sunk. The real trick was to know which of the logs of the dozens along the "perimeter of death" rolled as you stepped on them, causing you to lose your balance and fall to your toasty demise.

The building had a big steeple as many churches have, pointing the way to heaven where God lived, I guessed when He wasn't here. The pastor's office was next to the front entrance. Sometimes I looked in to see what he was doing—talking to God, reading? It was a mystery to me because a sheer white curtain shielded my view. I had to go in a few times to pick up papers for my Mom and was impressed with the enormous bookcases, large wooden desk, and big brown leather chair. Sitting in his office felt ominous as if I was sitting in a courtroom, anxiously waiting for the judge to enter.

The pastor, in accordance with Lutheran tradition, wore several layers of robes that flowed to the floor. The top layer was mostly white, and I think he wore a black shirt underneath because a black collar protruded. The robe had a long wide scarf that went almost to the floor on both sides. The scarf was green with a few gold symbols at the ends. Maybe it was because I was a kid, but when he walked out of his office right before the service, adorned with the long flowing robes, he looked larger than life, a friendly giant. He usually had a stern look about him, but sometimes he caught me looking at him and gave me a smile.

Worship services were held in the sanctuary. Its purpose originated from the Old Testament description of how God met and communicated with the High Priest, who in turn, conveyed to the people what God had told him. The High Priest was elected by the followers to represent them and go into the presence of God. He mediated for the sins of the people and himself by offering sacrifices and receiving instruction. Only the High Priest was allowed to enter and speak directly to God; the place was called the Holy of Holies and was where God physically resided at times. It was sectioned off from the rest of the sanctuary by a large curtain. If another person attempted to enter the Holy of Holies, they immediately were struck dead by God. To prevent any misfortune, sometimes the High

Priest was attached with a rope, so if he happened to die during the meeting with God, someone could pull him out with no risk to their lives.

This was a good depiction of the image of God. Certainly, He was all-powerful, knew everything, made everything, and could do anything. He was also inflexible on obedience and belief in him. Punishment, death, and hell were components of who God was, and in turn, respect, admiration, and worship was required if we wanted to survive. But this was not a bad thing for me because He would not invoke his wrath on us since we were Christians and we were Lutherans. Because of this, God was good to us and would guide us through all problems in life and then let us into heaven when we died.

When I spent time in the sanctuary and playing with friends on the church property, I had a sense of belonging mixed with a sense of apprehension; a strange tension that remained with me for many years. Before that, I developed my ideas about God in a typical way.

GOD—TAKE ONE

I was baptized as an infant in this Lutheran church. The purpose of baptism was to present me to God and a member of His church. This event occurred even though I could not understand what was going on. I questioned this practice when I was older. The answer was that my parents, along with the church family, raised me in the tradition of the church. As a Lutheran, we could say we were "born into the family of God." Other Protestant denominations do not agree with this, stating that only adult baptism is mentioned in the Bible, not infant baptism. Also, supporters of adult baptism believe that God wants each of us to knowingly commit to being a Christian, which cannot occur with infants.

As a child growing up in the Lutheran church, I went to Sunday school from preschool through high school to learn about the Bible and Jesus. In seventh and eighth grade, in addition to Sunday school, all Lutherans attended other special classes lead by the pastor on a weekday night for two years to study the finer points of the faith. The classes were organized this way so we could confirm our faith and became full members of the church at the end of the eight-grade. The process included reading and memorizing many statements written by Martin Luther about the Bible, scripture verses, and statements about the Lutheran faith.

"Wasn't he afraid that he would get in trouble?" asked a boy during one of our confirmation classes. He was referring to the Ninety-five Theses Martin Luther nailed to the Wittenberg Castle Catholic Church door in Germany on October 31, 1517. Martin Luther was the first of many reformers that challenged and broke away from the Catholic Church in the seventeenth century. This action was a response to intense oppression by the church that had gone unchecked for centuries.

"Yes, he did get into a lot of trouble with the church," replied the pastor. "Martin Luther was excommunicated from the Catholic Church." Luther's Ninety-five Theses provided the groundwork for many other groups of Catholics who "protested" the oppressive rule of the Church, initiating hundreds of denominations of "protestants" and the age of worldwide reformation.

The Catholic church offered spiritual remedies that could be obtained by giving money to the church and buying your way to good standing. Luther's point in this dramatic action was to remind all Christians that everyone was equal before God. The impositions the church placed on individuals were self-serving to maintain power and amass vast fortunes. The Catholic church began as a group of Christian followers that organized themselves and initiated a universal church. The word catholic, small "c" means universal. They heeded Jesus's announcement that his disciple Peter, whose name means "rock," would be the cornerstone of his church: "And upon this rock, I will build my church."

The members of this catholic church understood this statement meant that Peter was the head of the church, i.e., the first "Pope." The word Pope is from the Latin word "father" or "head of bishops," meaning overseers or watchers. This position had the unique attribute being able to convey God's word to the followers and was passed on through laying of hands from one to another consecutively through generations. This clearly distinguished this first group of Christian believers from all other groups by claiming they were able to trace their leadership to the first Christ-ordained leader, Peter. Thus, the transformation from catholic, small "c," to the Catholic Church, large "C."

From my perspective, many of us in my confirmation class didn't care a whole lot about confirmation. We just looked forward to the day we wouldn't have to go to classes during the week and miss essential TV shows. An added bonus was that we would be able to take communion once we had finished the classes. That was a big thing. Lutheranism was one of the few Protestant faiths that still used actual wine during communion. Many other churches switched to grape juice to avoid tempting those who had issues with alcohol. From time to time, my friends and I would sneak a look in the side closet where they kept the wine. Our church always bought Manischewitz, so the big news was when we were confirmed we could officially drink!

The idea of taking communion was to reaffirm that you were a part of Christ. This tradition was based on the Last Supper, right before Jesus was captured and killed. He shared his flesh and blood with his followers to demonstrate how connected they were. Many Catholics believe that the bread and wine in the service change into actual blood and flesh of Jesus called "transubstantiation." Most Protestants believe it to be a symbol.

The way you received communion was to walk to the front of the sanctuary and kneel at a wooden railing. The minister walked down the row of people and offered the "bread of Christ" and give you a thin white wafer. He immediately came by again, offering you the "blood of Christ," which was the wine in a glass close in size and shape to a shot glass. There we were doing shots of wine in church! This ritual was symbolic of Christ's physical suffering of his body, the bread, and his blood, the wine. I remember asking my mom if after we received the first shot if we could run down the line and get another. She smiled and told me she didn't think so.

Sunday worship services were organized with two activities going simultaneously, an early worship service starting around 8:30 a.m. and several Sunday school classes for both adults and children. When the first service ended, so did the first set of classes. After a short break, a second service began with another set of classes. So, for those going to Sunday school and the service, there was a break between the two. I didn't know the other kids that well, so hanging out with friends wasn't my first option. Our church was in a neighboring town of our school's archrival school, Roxbury High School, the nemesis of our existence. The two schools were competitive in almost all sports and drew tremendous crowds at athletic events. We had some time to kill between services, so many times I sat in the car to pass the time. This provided an opportunity for me to make an interesting discovery.

One year my mom got a brand-new Chevy Nova II. It was two-tone, red on the bottom, and white hardtop, pretty sporty for my mom. On Sundays between services, I retreated to the car, pretending to drive all over the world. One time, as I was winning some international race over the Andes, the radio turned on suddenly. I didn't have the keys, but the radio turned on by itself. And then it turned off. It took weeks of work trying to figure out how this was happening. Finally, I discovered that if I depressed the brake pedal, turned the directional signal to the left and hit the four-way hazard button, the radio turned on. Unbelievable. Months later, I asked a mechanic who was working on the car how that could happen. He said it was called induction. Apparently, when wires with no electric current are close to wires that have current, electricity transfers, or is inducted to the non-powered wires. The radio's wires pulled current from some combination of the brake, signal, and hazard light wiring. Finally, I had learned a practical lesson at church.

Little did I know, my passion for understanding God in a practical sense would follow me for the next fifty years.

THE GOOD, THE BAD, AND THE FAMILY

Because of my position in the family, I knew what to expect in many areas of life. I had two older brothers and a sister who warned me when bad things were going to happen. For example, I would not get ice cream after dinner if I didn't clean my room, or Dad would be mad if I didn't do my chores. They warned me about a lot of other things too, like what would happen if I didn't do what they wanted me to do, or what would happen if I didn't stop talking. Some threats were vague but got my attention.

My closest older brother in age, Glenn, is three years older than me, my second oldest brother, Lew, is seven years older, and my sister Kathy nine years older than me. Lew, or "Lewie" as we called him, was named after my dad, Lewis Jr., with Grampa being Lewis Sr. Sometimes, Granma called Lewie "Butch," but he didn't like that. Later in his life, Lewie wanted everyone to call him Lewis, and then shortly after that, he didn't want anyone to call him at all. He did not want what to be part of the family or communicate with us in any way. To respect his wishes, I will refer to him henceforth as "X."

X was quiet and kept to himself and his friends. After all, he was seven years older than me and to a kid that was a lifetime or two. I had the impression that X thought about things that Mom and Dad didn't think about. He took everything seriously. He was the first one in our family to say he was unsatisfied with the Lutheran church and wanted "more" from religion. Little did we know his thirst for more would transform our family's view of religion and spirituality.

Being the youngest could be tough, but it provided many advantages in the long run. The reason was that I usually became familiar with the issues, problems, and decisions my siblings had to deal with through the stages of growing up. I knew about milestone life events because being the youngest, anything I was dealing with had already happened three times before it was my turn. For example, when I began considering colleges, I visited at least five colleges with my siblings before I was thinking about school for myself. The same thing happened with sports, learning how to drive, and other life events. A negative consequence of being the youngest was that I was the family tag-along. To me, my older siblings always had more important things going on, and my life was not as important. I headed up the "been-there-done-that" department of our family. But I didn't feel I neglected to a great degree, Mom and Dad always made sure to include all of us in family events. There are pros and cons to each family position.

Years later, through the help of a counselor, I became aware of the deep and painful feelings I associated with being the youngest. Many times, I felt as if I was an appendage of the family rather than a valuable member. As a result, I developed the ability to detach and operate in my world to varying degrees. It seemed to me that family life was always about what was going on with my brothers and sister. Their issues were more grown-up, relevant, and urgent.

Kathy was and still is quite a headstrong and passionate person. Whatever she sets her mind on, she attacks with all her heart and defends it vehemently. One example of her enthusiasm was how she supported X, Glenn, and me in high school athletics. My brothers and I wrestled throughout high school, and whenever she came to a wrestling match to watch one of us, you could hear her voice over the crowd. "Get him, Glenn! Pin him!" I could even hear her rooting for me sometimes while I was wrestling. This was unusual since we had to wear headgear while wrestling, inhibiting outside noises, in addition to focusing on doing whatever I could to outmaneuver my opponent.

Another example relates to a string of discussions Kathy had with Mom when she was in high school about sewing small bells on the slip of her school clothes. It was in the 1960s, and all the girls were doing it, and Kathy had to be one of them. Oh, the arguments, over and over again.

"But *why* do you want to do this, Kathleen?" Mom asked, evoking her full name for added intensity.

"Because everyone has bells and I'll be one of the only ones without them!" Kathy pleaded.

Repeatedly asking "why" was Mom's only defense. Kathy had much more to lose socially, so she continued her demands with an unlimited amount of energy. Eventually, Mom succumbed, and Kathy went jingling off to school.

When we were young, serious family discussions were held in the kitchen with the door to the hallway closed. When the door was closed, you were isolated from whatever was going on in the kitchen. However, the door was one of those hollow-core types that did little to block sound. Many times, I crept to the end of the hallway or partially down the stairs to listen to what was going on. The stairway perch was best because I could quickly scamper up the steps and into the bathroom if someone opened the door suddenly. It was also closed when Kathy had friends over, and Mom and Dad were out.

One evening, when I was very young, Kathy was watching me because Mom and Dad went out with friends. I was going from the living room to the bathroom off the hallway, and I saw two friends of Kathy's kissing in the kitchen. To a kid, that was as repulsive as anything. When I gathered enough nerve up to exit the bathroom and return to the safety of the couch and TV, I noticed the door was shut. Who knew what was going on in there? Most likely, more kissing.

Glenn and I were buddies, especially in the early school years because Kathy and X were so much older. We did almost everything together. My life changed so much when he started elementary school, and I was stuck at home by myself with no one to play with. At some point in that three-year gap when Glenn began kindergarten, and before I started school, Mom let me walk halfway up to the bus stop and wait for him to come home. We lived on a dead-end street, so it was safe. There were only three houses on our street, each situated on the same side of the road. The first house was on the main road, the second was where my father's parents lived, and our house was third. Since my grandfather had the road put in and built the first two houses, he named the road after our family name "Guerin Lane." Opposite the houses were hundreds of acres of fields, usually containing meandering cows. I always thought Guerin Lane was two to three miles long until one of Glenn's friends told me I was an idiot and that it was only a quarter of a mile from our house to the main road. I walked halfway to the main road and stopped in front of my grandparent's house to wait for Glenn to come home from the school that robbed him from me during the days. I sat on one of several randomly shaped small boulders that made up the curb. Mostly, I sat and watched the cows eating grass and wandering through the field in no apparent direction. I thought they would get tired of eating grass day in and day out, but they didn't seem to mind.

    The fields adjacent to our house continued past our property for miles. Three-to-four-foot high stone walls separated the large areas of green. These were not neatly constructed walls of precisely picked and placed stone as seen in magazines. They were rows of gray shoebox-sized boulders with small groups of trees sprouting up periodically. Glenn and I went on many adventures across these fields, climbing the stone dividers and searching through the occasional stand of trees. He always took the lead. After all, Glenn was three years older than me and knew tons more. He took me under his wing, with many commenting that he was such a good big brother. And I agreed. The one thing I didn't realize was behind his altruistic intentions was also an undercurrent of control. He initiated many of the things we did, and I pretty much had to follow along. Not to say that he didn't think of me, but it was more his choice than mine when we decided to do things. For some reason, he had a strong desire to win at everything.

It took me years to see how his dominating influence affected me and how I adjusted by pursuing my interests in sports, friends, and then later in life with religion and spirituality.

DAD, A CORRELATE OF GOD

Dad was the head of the house; there was no doubt about that. By the time I came into the family, he had launched his own trucking business, a venture he'd had to fight his father to start.

Dad grew up on his father's dairy farm. A few years after high school, he decided he didn't want to run the farm and wanted to do something else. Dad wanted to start a trucking company. It came to a head one day, and he and his dad had a huge argument, leaving Dad upset for months. He eventually started the trucking company out of our house, which was, unfortunately, next door to his parents. There was always a level of friction when he and his dad interacted. Not too many big arguments, but uneasy feelings were plentiful when we got together.

One Christmas morning, they had a gigantic fight. We were opening presents the morning after attending the midnight Christmas Eve service. Those services should be considered torture. They were late at night, we were tired, and Christmas was the next day. The minutes ticked on like hours. One of the only exciting things that happened was when we were allowed to hold a small candle when we sang *Silent Night* at the end of the service. At the end of the song, we blew them out and went home. Presents coming soon!

Anyway, that Christmas morning, the magical atmosphere of opening gifts was shattered with Dad slamming the phone and pounding down the hall toward us in a rage. The cows had gotten out of their field, and Grampa wanted help to corral them back immediately. He told Dad to "get the kids" and come and help him. Dad was furious

"On Christmas day, for God's sake!" he bellowed. Dad, X, and Kathy went to coax the walking slabs of beef back into the barn. I was too young to go, so I stayed home and played with my new Flintstones Dino the Dinosaur play-action toy.

At times, Dad was an unpredictable keg of gun powder. Never abusive, but wow, did he get angry. We were all afraid of what "your father is going to do when he gets home," as my mom often said. He was the disciplinarian, the enforcer, the one you were afraid of. He didn't even have to do anything; you did not want to risk it to see what would happen when he got mad. One memorable glimpse occurred one night after dinner.

Glenn and I were playing with a pair of those plastic suctioned-cupped dart guns. We were allowed to have these toy guns as long as we did not, under any circumstances, shoot each other in the face or head. Typically, as we played with the guns, we lost all the darts except one. In these instances, I shot the lone dart at him, and then he would load it, and shoot it back at me. Of course, we were aiming at whatever part of the body we saw; arms, legs, or heads. As usual, Dad was in the living room, reading the paper, and watching TV.

That night, Glenn and I were shooting it out in the dining room and adjoining kitchen which was separated on one side by a doorway into the hall. The dart flew back and forth past the doorway, sometimes falling to the floor, sometimes sticking to the cabinet, and occasionally hitting one of us. On one exchange, he shot at me and missed. My next shot aimed and shot just as he headed between the refrigerator and counter. Bam, right in the ear. An excellent shot!

"Owwwa...you just missed my eye!" He said, laughing so hard he could barely breathe, while at the same time reloading his gun. But something deep inside sent a message to my conscious mind that these words were not good. But it was too late.

"I told you two to *never* shoot at each other in the face!" Came the booming voice from the living room, followed by giant footsteps coming down the hallway. The water in the pots and pans soaking in the sink shook like the water-filled footprints in *Jurassic Park*. My quick-thinking brother thought the best way to avoid any negative consequences was not to get caught red-handed, so he tossed me his gun and said: "Here, take this!" My first mistake was to catch the gun; my second mistake was far more serious. Moments later, Dad entered the room, his face contorted almost beyond recognition with anger, his brow furrowed, and his eyes squinted.

"Why do you two keep doing this when I told you not to?" he roared. Time slowed to a crawl. Everything felt like it was in slow motion. Dad looked at Glenn, who was in a state of paralysis, only his eyes blinking. I had a moment to think. Then I got it, a great defense. Go with it.

"Dad, we were just pretending," I said with remarkable made-up candor. "The guns aren't even loaded." With that, I lifted the gun in my hand and aimed at Dad. "See?" and squeezed the trigger. As I did this, I sensed it had some resistance, which was odd because when the gun didn't have a dart in it, there was no resistance. Uh oh. Then, with that familiar soft click and slight kick-back, the dart launched out of the plastic barrel. As it flew toward my father, I suddenly remembered that Glenn had loaded his gun before he tossed it to me. I had instinctively put my unloaded gun on the counter and caught his. Unfortunately, my mind didn't register the switch until the moment I pulled the trigger. Oh My God. The dart hit Dad right in the forehead!

What happened next was a blur. The dart bounced off Dad's head, and by the time it hit the floor, Glenn was out of the room, leaving me to die alone. I barely remember him running out. It was one of those blurs of color like in the movies when a superhero moves extremely fast. Dad turned his gaze to me and took a step closer. He exploded. Although Dad never hit us, when he got angry, it was obvious he was mad. His entire body tensed, and his stare ratcheted up to such an intense level, he could stare down a wild animal. All of this made you think something terrible was about to happen. We didn't know what, but it would be bad.

Paralyzed with fear, I automatically resorted to my most effective defensive maneuver. Many times, I used it halfheartedly to avoid punishment or to retaliate against an assault from one of my older siblings. I never felt good about using it, but in this case, it was warranted. This called for a few manufactured tears.

IF IT'S NOT ONE THING, IT'S YOUR MOTHER

Supposedly, Freud coined this phrase which probably originated from the intense emotional bonds seen between mothers and their children. A bond less frequently seen in father/child relationships, especially before the 80s when dads got involved in caregiving.

My mom and I were no different. Mom told me a few times that I came to into this world after she and Dad thought they enjoyed my brothers and sister so much, they decided to have one more child. She began to tell me one day, "It was a beautiful summer night at the shore in September when..."

"No, no, no!" I said, cupping my hand over my ears. That was getting to be way too much information. The point is that I was lucky enough to be born to parents that knew they wanted to have one more child even after having three others. Unless of course, they kept trying to see if they could raise the perfect child. If they were, I'm not sure if they succeeded.

My mom is an organizer. She always wanted everything planned in the best way possible. She used to say, "This way, everything that has to get done, will get done." As a result, growing up in our house, there were numerous lists, plans, and schedules. The good thing was that throughout my life, I can see how this helped me learn to organize and execute projects. The bad thing was that when kids are raised this way, skills of self-reliance and self-direction can be underdeveloped.

As far as I knew, Mom was the same as my friend's moms. If I wanted a friend to come over or to go to someone's house, we asked our moms, and they arranged the days and times. She reacted as predicted to certain things too. For example, one warm fall day, my friend Johnny and I went on a hike through the fields behind my house. We followed the stone walls to the woods, two fields back to a stream near the southern property line. We were floating short pieces of sticks in the stream, racing them as if they were speed boats in a raging and dangerous river. Then we got bored. What else could we do? Hmm.

"I know," said Johnny, "we can make small rafts and float them down the stream."

"Even better," I said, "we can pile leaves on them and light them on fire as they go down."

"That's a great idea!" Johnny said, "Did you bring matches?"

"No, but I'll run back and get them while you build the boats."

I ran full speed back to the house so fast I surprised myself. All the while, I was thinking about our "flaming racing boat" scenario. This was going to be great! I could see it now, flaming boats tearing down the rapids racing each other while dodging rocks and logs. I ran across the front yard and saw Mom at the kitchen sink watching me.

"What's going on, Scott? Is Johnny alright?" she looked at me with a concerned face as I exploded through the screen door. Of course, she'd wonder why I hit the porch at break-neck speed and without Johnny.

"Johnny's fine," I said, barely getting the words out between breaths.

"We, we're ..." I said panting, "making rafts, and, and," more panting, "we thought it would be fun to build rafts and set them on fire and race them." I pulled open the drawer right by the door, searching through it with both my hand and my eyes.

But just as I said it, it hit me. This is not the type of thing you tell your mom.

"No, you are *not* going anywhere with matches, especially in the woods!" Mom declared with so much conviction and anger; it seemed pointless to try to change her mind. But I had to try.

"Oh, Mom! We were only going to set them on fire while they're in the stream, and Johnny is down there now waiting for me." I said this with as much pleading in my voice as I could muster.

"I said no!" she said with even more power. "And don't ever ask me again about bringing matches into the woods." She stormed out of the kitchen.

I stopped for a moment and thought about reaching in the drawer and taking a book of matches. But one of Mom's superpowers was knowing what we were doing no matter where she was. Mom had said many times she had "eyes in the back of her head." This concerned me. I could only imagine what would happen if she caught me taking the matches. It wasn't worth it.

Johnny, of course, gave me the expected response when I returned.

"You idiot! You never, under any circumstances, tell your mom you are going to play with matches. Never."

We resumed our scaled-down white water adventure without any fire effects. It was still a fun day overall.

Mom was the one to make sure we said grace before dinner and our prayers at night. If you said your prayers too fast, she made you say them slower. Not Dad. He'd come in, you shot off the prayer, and he was out.

Mom was also the one to get us up and out to church on Sundays. She was more committed to the ritual than Dad. From time to time one of my brothers or Kathy would go a few rounds of the "Why do we have to go to church?" objection only to be countered with a few responses, "to get to know God" or "so you will be a good Lutheran." Round 1, round 2, and then the knock-out statement, "Because I said so." End of discussion. Get in the car.

Our first images of God, many times, are based on who our parents are; how they express their love and support, or not; how they discipline us, or not; and how they relate to each other, or not. My overall first impression was of love and concern, but as typical of families in the 60s and 70s, there was a heavy authoritarian influence. That matched how I thought of God. He's around, cares for us; but don't get too close, don't ask too much, and most of all, BE GOOD.

THERE'S GOT TO BE SOMETHING ELSE

Religion was something we had to do. In the Lutheran church, the entire service was scripted, from the opening hymn to the escape to the car. One part of the service that always bugged me was the group reciting during the worship service. Even as a kid, I could never understand how people could read scripture in a monotone, lifeless way. The verses contained exciting things that foretold of tremendous promises about salvation, forgiveness, and God's love, yet they were spoken as if they were instructions on how to change a flat tire. Always repeated in lower tones than usual, the sedative murmurings would match in cadence and go on and on and then abruptly stop. I always got a kick out of the people who didn't pay attention, so when everyone else stopped reciting, a lone voice or two would continue, "and the next day..." and then sharply end with embarrassment. Well, at least I was embarrassed for them because it happened to me a few times too.

Going to church was like school. In a way, it was better, because it didn't go all day, but in another, it was worse because it was on the weekend, and I had to get dressed up in a suit and tie. I swear I never had a shirt that didn't practically choke me with the top button buttoned. The whole morning was uncomfortable and long. I don't know if it was just my perception, but it seemed to me that our entire family was unhappy about going, and after we got home, everyone was on edge. I spent many Sunday afternoons staying away from everyone because arguments would inevitably erupt. Me, being the youngest, bore the brunt of the "trickle-down" effect.

Despite the resistant feelings about going to church and enduring the seemingly day-long sermons, I had an ambient interest in God. Don't get me wrong; I was not some prepubescent sage holding study groups at recess. In general, going to church was boring, and there was lots of clock-watching on my part. But something was nagging at me, causing me to wonder what was behind all of it. Where would I get the answers? I could read the Bible, but it was hard to read, and I wasn't sure what it meant. The only other option I could think of was to learn as much as I could from the people that knew something. My parents were the first to admit they didn't know much about religion or the Bible. It's not that they were unintelligent; they preferred to leave those things to the church. The only person I knew who could answer my questions was my pastor, and luckily, he was teaching the confirmation classes. The timing was perfect since I was entering the seventh grade and starting confirmation classes.

The classes began, and everything was going well. I was absorbing all the content with no difficulty. As I mentioned earlier, I even started one of the confirmation requirements a year early by taking sermon notes. Little did I know, doing that lead to the spark where I began my greatest journey.

ENTER SIN

Sin was a tough thing to figure out as a kid. On the one hand, it was looming darkness all around. Sin was in the world and everyone. On the other hand, it was supposed to be kept at bay by going to church and trying to be good. In the end, only bad people went to hell, and whatever that was, it would be a terrible experience. At least those were my first impressions of sin. We sinned when we gave in to selfishness or were bad. When people screamed and fought, when people stole, and the cops got them, and when people are mean, that's all sin. The Ten Commandments told us what was right and wrong; don't steal, kill, disobey mom and dad, and worship God at all times. The rule was to be good, coupled with the old "Do unto others as you would have them do unto you."

As a kid, I remember thinking the commandments were mostly common sense even if it was hard at times to keep them. Don't throw sticks at people. Don't play with your brothers' or sister's stuff unless they said it was okay. Don't lie. Do whatever Mom and Dad said. And go to church. I noticed the commandments had earthly applications as well. If I misbehaved and got caught, I suffered the consequences of the wrath of my siblings or Mom's weighty sentence of "Go to your room until your father gets home." Either option was scary. Glenn's wrath was swift and painful, Mom's was long and drawn-out waiting, waiting, waiting for Dad. Many times, Mom came up to my room before he came home to say that it was okay to come out, sometimes after a short talk about not doing it again. This is where I learned the value of "fake penance," where a sad face or a teary look turned things around quickly. I felt bad about using this tactic, but it worked in a pinch.

As far as the eternal consequences of sin, I didn't think about it much. Who thought about "eternity?" Only old people died anyway. Although, if pressed, I think most kids have some sense of eternity, and it was defined as doing anything they didn't want to do for more than half an hour.

Overall, I felt okay because I was going to church and not killing people. I figured the pastor and the other church leaders would defend me if someone wanted to know if I was going to heaven or not. I couldn't see any reason to be sent to hell. I was a pretty good kid, well, other than the fake tears. I knew occasionally I technically didn't follow the commandments. I stole stuff from my brothers and sister. I lied to get out of things, and sometimes I got angry at Mom and Dad. I certainly didn't kill anyone, and I knew for sure that ants and bugs were excluded, mainly because they were ants and bugs. So, I assumed I would go to heaven one day just like everyone else as long as I didn't screw up.

GOD AND FAMILY

Our concept of the world expands out from a center in circles as we mature. Developmental psychologists tell us that infants initially perceive no difference between them and their immediate caregivers. Their world is one symbiotic relationship. It's all "me" at birth and for many months after. As an infant child matures, they perceive there is an "other." They become aware that there is someone else out there interacting with them. They begin to recognize caregivers coming and going, feeding them, or speaking to them, and begin to sense a separation. It's important to note that during these early years, the concept of whether the world is a safe place or a hurtful place, is indelibly imprinted.

Gradually the circle expands, and our world begins to include extended family, siblings, grandparents, and cousins. Then our awareness increases to the community level when we enter the school-age years and meet other children and families. Even broader perspectives are created when we learn about other countries and cultures; the most significant perspective is our concept of the world and God. So, just as a pebble dropped into a still pond creates expanding and rippling circles, so do our circles of awareness. Most importantly, what we experience at each stage will shape our perspective of the world, of ourselves, and our concept of God.

My initial concept of God was heavily influenced by how I experienced my parents and my family. My dad was the somewhat distant authoritarian, the head of the house, the one you didn't mess with. But he could also be the jokester. My mom represented the nurturing part of God and the organizer, the planner of plans not easily altered. She always had dinner organized, and lunches made for me to take to school. She gave me rides to friend's houses and picked me up after school.

A good description of what our family was like could be seen in the families depicted in the movie *A Christmas Story* or the TV series *The Wonder Years*. We aren't exactly like them, but similar. From what I saw, my friends' families were much the same. Parenting styles before the 70s were authoritarian invoking the "children should be seen and not heard" approach. In later years parenting models transitioned to be more relational, providing more opportunities for the child to express themselves and discuss issues with their parents. The good thing about the earlier style was that children were raised with a sense of fear of authority that invoked discipline and order. The bad thing was that children did not develop self-expression or feel comfortable being themselves. The relational style has its positives and negatives also. The good thing is that children are encouraged to be themselves, express their feelings, and what they want to do. However, the negative is a lack of respect for parents, authority, and low self-reliance.

My dad's interest in God and the church was not outwardly evident. As I mentioned, we all went to church on Mom's prodding because that is the way it was. And we offered grace before our dinner each night. Another glimpse of the way my dad was reflected was in what he did just before the assigned family member recited the blessing:

"God is great; God is good; now we thank him for this food. Amen."

This was one of the times where the fun side of Dad appeared. For some time, we had a record player in the dining room just within Dad's reach. This was a console unit about the size of a small bookcase. The left side was fabric and concealed the speakers. The right side had a few dials and a clear plastic start button that protruded about an inch from the cabinet.

Dad's favorite musical genre was jazz, especially Peggy Lee, who had several hit songs in the 1960s. Right after one of us was told to say grace and as we were all bowing our heads and folding our hands, Dad would blurt out "Wait!" and with a wonderful glint in his eye, lean over and push the start button. Unseen from the outside, the turntable started spinning, the armature containing the needle rose from its cradle, and the record, perched on a metal stem, dropped on the spinning turntable. The armature swung back over the record, gently lowered to the outer edge of the disk and began playing. The entire mechanical process took about ten seconds - the exact amount of time it took to say grace. So, as long as the person started as Dad pushed the button, the moment after "Amen," the deep sultry voice of Ms. Lee would fill the room. We all snickered a bit when Mom glared at Dad across the table.

WING AND A PRAYER

When I was growing up, praying was mainly reciting statements. For example, saying grace at dinner time. The one I recited thousands of times before going to bed was:

> "Jesus dear, be real near, nothing then I need fear. God bless Mommy, and Daddy, Kathy, Butch, and Glenn, Granma and Grampa, Nana and Grampa John, and everybody. Amen."

Corny. I remember feeling funny calling Jesus "dear," but I went along with it. I felt too that it was good to expand the blessing to "everybody," just in case someone was left out. Sometimes, individual names or requests were included if a friend or someone we knew needed something special or was sick.

In general, prayer was a Christmas list. I composed my list and sent it off, but never knew what, if any part of it, would be fulfilled. Requests went out to heaven, and God would consider them and decide if He would grant them, or not. I never expected to get everything on my list and always got things I never asked for, some good, some boring.

When I was around seven or eight years old, I conducted my first experiment in prayer. I was a kid, and I wanted toys, so the focus of this study concerned how to get an electric car. These were the first ride-in cars that could go a few miles an hour. They were made to look like real cars with doors that opened, authentic-looking plastic tires, and a plastic windshield, complete with working wipers. I wanted one desperately. It was all I thought about. I brought it up one night during dinner to see what Mom and Dad thought about them because I was thinking about asking for one for my birthday. Knowing they were expensive, I thought they could combine it with my Christmas present. It was a great idea. I could see myself driving it to my friends' houses, to school, and church, of course. Everyone would want to be my friend.

"Are you kidding?" Dad barked. "For crying out loud, those things are expensive." I never knew what he meant by that "for crying out loud" phrase he sometimes used, but knew it was serious and used in non-negotiable situations, as in it's over, don't bring it up again.

Oh great. Now I'll never get my electric car, I thought. Then it came to me, why don't I ask God? I was sure He would want me to have one. Why not? He gives us all good things; I'd heard it many times at church. So, one night after my regular prayer with Mom, I quietly asked God. "Dear God, please give me an electric car. I'll share it with anyone who asks me. Amen." The next morning, I remembered I had prayed about the car. I looked around the room. Nothing.

"Stupid, it's too big to be up here. It's got to be outside." I got dressed and went downstairs and immediately checked the garage. Nothing. It wasn't there.

"What are you looking for Scott?" Mom asked as I came back into the kitchen. "Nothing," I said sadly and made myself a bowl of Captain Crunch cereal. That always cheered me up.

Repetition, I thought. You have to say a prayer repeatedly to make it happen. God gets lots of prayers each day, so you have got to keep asking, and sooner or later, he will get around to you. Night after night, I said the same prayer, and day after day, nothing happened.

"That's it." I thought. "I'm going to take my business elsewhere." God was doing the authoritarian parent thing, and I was not happy. "I'll ask the Devil," I thought. "He always gives kids what they want." I thought this might be true from the scenes in Pinocchio where wayward boys were taken to Pleasure Island amusement park, where they could eat, drink, smoke, and do anything they wanted. The boys had a great time but then turned into donkeys. Hmm, maybe that could happen to me. But what the heck, I decided to try anyway.

"Mr. Devil, please give me an electric car, I don't care what color, but I want it bad. Amen." The next day, nothing. And that was the end of the electric car.

Although this childish experiment resulted in no results, what I didn't know then was decades later, I would spend several years conducting prayer research in my doctoral dissertation.

GETTING SERIOUS

I looked up to my oldest brother, X. Being seven years older, he was light years ahead of me in school, sports, and life in general. He was old enough to have a dog, a German Shepard named King, and all of X's friends were cool. But I knew he was a little different too. He was quiet and serious about everything. Even Dad joked around now and then, but X rarely did. He was like the older brother, Wally, on *Leave it to Beaver*, but not as warm and friendly.

It was X that started our family thinking differently about church. Because he took everything seriously, he began to question why we went to the Lutheran church. He couldn't stand to go through the motions of attending services week after week singing familiar songs and reciting passages penned by Luther. I don't know precisely when or how his objections began. At some point, he let Mom and Dad know that he wanted to attend a group that met on Friday nights that had fun and studied the Bible. They didn't object, and he went regularly. Now and then X and my parents had discussions, sometimes heated, about why he didn't want to go to the Lutheran church and wanted to spend time with his Friday night group instead. The only thing I caught from these discussions, held behind the closed kitchen door, was that he didn't get anything out of going to church and he learned more about God in this other group. They allowed him to go to his group as long as he continued to go to our church as well.

X's misgivings stirred my thinking as well. I already knew that going to church was not on my top-ten list, but not going was unthinkable. But his words about "getting something out of" going to church nagged at me. This prompted me to pay more attention in church. Confirmation classes started, so I decided to try to learn something in class. Well, that was harder to do than I thought.

Confirmation classes were always on a weeknight. I was usually tired, and the only way to keep things interesting was to fool around making jokes and scheming how to throw the kids from our neighboring and rival school, Roxbury, in the bushes during the break. Those of us from my hometown school, Randolph, inevitably started talking during our 15-minute break about the big game coming up or one that had just occurred. Occasionally, the Roxbury kids entered the discussion, and things escalated to pushing and shoving. That's when we ended up throwing a few of them in the low shrubs that lined the side of the building. It helped that none of them were athletes, and we were all wrestlers and football players. One time we all got in trouble for it and break time was temporally suspended.

Part of the preparation of being confirmed required us to take notes on the Sunday sermons and hand them to the pastor. This requirement always occurred in eighth grade, the second year of the two-year confirmation process. In the Catholic tradition, the sermon is the part of the service called the homily and, in both cases, it is a monologue usually conducted by a pastor or priest. It typically involves a scripture verse or Bible story, including practical applications. For some reason, Catholic homilies were short; my guess was about 15-20 min in total, which was great. Protestant sermons vary from 20 min to an hour or more depending on the church. As a kid, I swore they went on for days. But it was an effective way to learn about the Bible and how it was supposed to fit into our lives, especially if the pastor was a good speaker. Many times, I needed something to do during the services, so I decided to take notes on the sermons the first year. However, instead of throwing them out, I kept them.

BORN AGAIN

The religious group X went to was called Life Anew. It was not a part of any church or denomination but run by a group of people who lived in surrounding towns. X took Glenn there a few times, and Glenn enjoyed it, so I got up the nerve to go. The meetings were held in a building that looked like a barn. It was a new building built with donations of the group members, and they called it The Barn. It was one big, brightly lit room. Most of the time, it had a volleyball net set up in the center. That was the best thing about going there. I loved volleyball, and we played for hours. Many times, at the end of the evenings, when all the amateurs were done playing, we brought out a large and heavy ball and played until we were exhausted.

After some time of playing and visiting, we were served cookies and juice. We then all sat down on the concrete floor and listened to a talk about sections of the Bible and what they meant. The talk was the same as a sermon and most times someone led the group in song before the talk. The songs were not the ones we sang in church. They handed out sheets of paper, so we had the words. One thing that made these songs different wasn't that they were just about Jesus. They emphasized how good it was to be a Christian in more understandable words compared to the old fashioned hymns we sang in the Lutheran church. The songs indicated these people were in direct communication with God or Jesus. Some of the verses were:

> "And he walks with me, and he talks with me, and tells me I am His own . . ."
>
> "Sitting at the feet of Jesus, wondrous words I hear him say . . ."
>
> "What a friend we have in Jesus . . ."

Did they actually hear him and talk with him? I wondered.

Most of the people at the Life Anew meetings were different than those at my church. The group was usually around 30 people, and they were outgoing, funny, and joked with each other more than I ever saw at my church. I thought maybe it was because there weren't any older people there, but I wasn't sure. Initially, it seemed there was something wrong with people being fun and normal at a religious meeting. I thought people worshiping God were supposed to be somber and serious. That was a striking difference, the lack of formality even in clothing. Everyone there wore normal clothes; shorts, tee shirts, and sneakers.

The leader of the group was more solemn than the rest of the members. His name was Robert. He was a middle-aged large-framed man with black wavy hair and broad shoulders. He had a quiet and intense demeanor which immediately reminded me of X. I didn't feel comfortable approaching him. He always said hello to me and sometimes played on my side of the volleyball net. He was a good player. When he taught at the breaks, he spoke with authority. He knew the Bible and the nature of God. When studying one passage, he always referred to many other parts as well and related what he was talking about to everyday life. When people spoke about him, they did so with a level of respect or reverence, saying his name almost in a whisper. This seemed strange to me. It was one thing to be quiet and unapproachable, but several people seemed to revere him in a way that elevated him to an untouchable level.

A few times, when it was time to take a break from volleyball and start the snacks, the women would ask things like, "Is Robert ready yet?" Another would reply, "No, Robert is still preparing," and then another "Let me know when Robert comes out of the study, and I will call everyone to sit." They treated him as a spiritual guru or something.

"Who was this guy?" I thought . . . then went for the cookies.

Just as the songs and the attitude were different from my church, so were the teachings. The main difference between this group and my church was they focused on the idea of "knowing" Jesus and having a "relationship" with him. Now and then they spoke about nominal Christians. Nominal Christians believe in the Bible and Jesus and church, but Jesus didn't mean that much to them. I knew if I had to pick, I was probably a nominal Christian. I felt terrible about that and hoped no one in the group would ever discover it. These people said they were not just Christians; they were "born again" Christians. This was quite different from what I knew about religion. Everyone seemed to understand what it meant too. Many nodded their heads in agreement or added to what Robert was saying. I, on the other hand, had no idea what they were talking about. How could you "know" Jesus? He was not here. Yes, he came alive again at Easter, but he was not around now. But it was like these people believed he was alive now. This was an extraordinary difference. It was refreshing and disturbing at the same time. Wherever this was coming from, I did not know, but it got me thinking.

THE "NON" DENOMINATION

The differences I saw between Life Anew and my church were so vast it seemed impossible to reconcile the two. It was like two trains were heading towards each other on the same track. Worshiping God was either trying to be a good person and do the "Lutheran thing," or that was no good, and you had to do the "Jesus is alive thing." I didn't know much about what the people at The Barn were saying, but it was drastically different than what I knew. It seemed a little dangerous because it wasn't part of a *real* church. I might have picked that idea up from the discussions Mom and Dad had with X, but it made sense. How was one supposed to know which to pick? And what were the consequences if you chose wrong? Was there a wrong choice? I had to find out.

My first thought was to ask my parents, but I felt pretty sure I already knew what they thought about it from my stairway listening post. They didn't have a strong objection, but they were concerned. Either way, I needed more information and another source. For some reason, the dichotomy of belief systems loomed large in my mind. Don't get me wrong; I wasn't going into the desert fasting for weeks, looking for a burning bush. I was still doing kid stuff, playing around with my friends. But I did regularly mull the concept around in my mind.

Then, something else happened to complicate matters.

Several months after X brought up the Life Anew group, and we all adjusted, Glenn mentioned that he wanted to go to another church. But this was different. While Life Anew was not a church and we could go to both, Glenn wanted to go to another church altogether. It was called Bethlehem Church, and they held Sunday services in a real church building. I thought it was going to be a bigger deal to Mom and Dad than it ended up being. But I think they allowed it because he was confirmed. Glenn had a couple of other connections that had an influence too. His girlfriend's dad was the pastor, and he was friends with two of the pastor's sons. This church did not belong to any denomination, Protestant or Catholic. This church congregation fell into the category of "non-denominational" they were not a part of any larger national or international organization. They were self-funded, selected their pastors, and determined their own theological beliefs, which usually aligned with the Evangelical Christian beliefs.

Bethlehem Church was a modern church building rather than the traditional Lutheran Church nestled in the picture-postcard setting. This church had a dark wood and brick exterior with a large stained-glass window in the front and a steeple on top, again pointing the way to God. The building was positioned on a hill right off the two-lane highway. One great thing was that it was next door to a Dairy Queen. Glenn brought me to Bethlehem Church not too long after he started attending. I couldn't go on Sundays until after I was confirmed, the same deal they made with Glenn. So, I went there for social events and an occasional Sunday service.

No robes. That was strange. That's what struck me the first time I went to a Sunday morning worship service at Bethlehem Church. Neither the pastor nor other leaders wore robes. They just wore suits and dresses. There weren't many banners or cloth panels hanging around with symbols on them either. It was just a nicely decorated interior with a raised platform in the front with a single wooden podium. There was an organ on the left side, slightly lower than the stage.

The pastor was an outgoing, young-looking man in good physical condition, with light brown neatly trimmed hair, and piercing eyes. He came across with high energy, excitement in his voice, and a firm handshake. He exuded so much confidence I was startled. He was so different from my Lutheran pastor. The pastor's oldest son was just as outgoing, but I disliked him immediately. To me, he had a chip on his shoulder and thought he was better than everyone else, confident and smug. The pastor's younger son and daughter were much nicer people to be around.

Bethlehem Church had more than a head pastor. They also had a youth minister on staff. His name was William, and he was a "piece of work" as my dad would say. He was young as well, always had messy hair, and a constant smile. Both he and his wife were musicians, and William and his guitar were inseparable. Sometimes we met at the church on a Saturday and take a van to the Jersey shore for the day. When someone else was driving, William took out his guitar and led everyone in some of the same songs I heard at Life Anew. He also made up goofy songs about something we saw on the trip or made up lyrics poking fun at someone in the group.

William was a guy that seemed to enjoy keeping everyone guessing what he would do next. On Sunday mornings, if he had to make an announcement, many times he would say, "I was supposed to talk about the upcoming trip, but I have something else to say first." Then he would convey some unrelated story. He was not like any of the other leaders I knew. William's personality and actions provided a different perspective as I was sorting out my feelings about God, church, and the non-Lutheran issue. He was a genuine and personable guy who seemed to care about people genuinely, but he was also fun and wacky.

A funny thing relating to William happened a few years later, during my first year in college, when I began going to a non-denominational Christian group on campus. We were participating in an introductory meeting with all freshmen, and as an ice breaker, the group leaders wheeled in a green, two-sided chalkboard. One of the leaders, Dan, explained that in this exercise, we would share characteristics of people who had a significant impact on our relationship with God, and he wrote them on the board. As expected, some people offered words like "understanding," "compassionate," and "patient." As the students gave their answers, Dan wrote them on the front of the board. At the same time, another one of the leaders, Dale, was writing on the back of the board. I thought it was strange and wondered what he was writing. This went on for a while, and almost everyone offered an answer with many providing several, except me. When I realized this, my stomach churned, and my body tensed. It appeared everyone was looking at me.

"Let's hear from someone we haven't heard from yet," Dan said, scanning the room. Oh God. Quick, think of something. All the good answers were already taken. Crap. My mind was racing. I remembered thinking about William and how he was different from all the other religious leaders, signing those silly songs that had us all laughing. I thought about the time when we stopped at a rest stop to get gas, and he hauled us out of the 15-passenger van to play "buck-buck" a game where one person jumped on another one at a time until we all collapsed into one big laughing pile.

Another time we were on the way to a retreat in the same van and passed acres of rolling green pastures with several cows on the side of a steep hill grazing. William went into a long and serious discourse of how these cows were called "hillside" cows because the front and rear legs on the uphill side were shorter than the two on the downside. They were specially grown this way so that farmers could plant grass on hills and have cows able to eat, therefore, making the best use of the land. These cows, of course, could never walk on flat ground because they toppled over, so special barns were constructed on the sides of the hills, also following the steep contour of the land. We didn't see any of the special barns, but it seemed plausible. Not too long after that, someone, probably one of my brother's friends, told me I was an idiot to think that there was such a thing as hillside cows.

"How about you?" Dan said pointedly, looking right at me, along with everyone else in the room. "What characteristic of a person that you know was important to your understanding of God?"

"Well," I said tentatively, "I guess the best word to describe my youth pastor, uh, would be, crazy." A split second after I offered my reply, Dale popped his head out from behind the board, just as soft laughter filled the room.

"Crazy, Hum, that's interesting." said Dan as a smile broke across his face." Dale was not happy with my response and shook his head. A few moments passed with no one doing anything, Dan and Dale looked at each other. Laughter and an air of uncertainty held the room "Now wait a minute," said Dan. "It's his answer." Reluctantly, Dale stepped behind the board and wrote briefly.

"Ok," said Dan. "We have asked you to give us the characteristics of people that have been important in your understanding of what God was like. Now we will show you how the answers are characteristics of Jesus." Dan and Dale went to each end of the board and slowly spun it entirely around, so the back of the board was now visible. Someone had, prior to the meeting, wrote columns of identical words and a line immediately after. During the session while the Dan was writing the one-word characteristic on the front, Dale was writing the same word in the blank completing the phrase, so it looked like this:

Jesus is <u>loving</u>
Jesus is <u>patient</u>
Jesus is <u>understanding</u>
Jesus is <u>a good listener</u>
And then my answer:
Jesus is <u>crazy</u>

There were a few moments of silence and then all-out, loud laughter. Dan must have sensed I was embarrassed by the laughter. He broke through the noise with a loud voice saying, "Well, everyone can certainly say that Jesus was much different than everyone else in his day. He was a rebel, he confronted the Jewish leadership, and many most likely thought he was crazy." That was a great way to place my answer into perspective.

Both the Life Anew and Bethlehem Church groups were considered non-denominational Christian groups. They were Christian because their focus was on Jesus, and they studied the Judeo-Christian Bible. They followed the teaching of the Old Testament held by the Jewish religion, but also believed that Jesus came from the Jewish culture to become the savior of the world. The organizational difference was they did not belong to any of the established Christian denominations as with Catholicism, Presbyterian, Methodist, and Lutheran. Each of these groups has its own rules, regulations, and traditions developed over several hundred years. Non-denominational churches could worship God whatever way they wanted with no overriding organizational structure. Many pride themselves that they do not get lost in religious dogma and teach strictly what the Bible says.

THE FLAME

I was still in eighth grade, X was in college, and I was struggling with the two different approaches to God. I wondered if one was better than the other, the Lutheran approach, or Life Anew? No matter how much I thought about it, I could not come to any conclusion. I began the second year of confirmation classes that included the requirement to take sermon notes to submit for grading. During the first class of the year, the pastor was explaining the note-taking requirement, and suddenly it hit me. Why didn't I think of it before? I could ask him about Life Anew and their approach to the Bible. I could tell him about the differences I noticed and ask him what to do. He would give me the information I needed.

An Ah-Ha moment. Finally, I could get the help I needed. My mind raced. How should I ask? Just bring it up? Would I just go right up to him and ask him about this other group? Would he get mad at me? I wasn't sure how to do it, but I knew this was the way to go. I could bring it up when handing in the sermon notes. That was an excellent opportunity, the perfect time to ask. I could say I had a question about the sermons. Even better, I could bring in the sermon

ANGEL IN TRAINING

notes from last year. He would be impressed I had begun taking notes a year before we were required. We could start with a discussion about the sermon notes, and then I would bring up my Life Anew questions. I had a plan.

I was reviewing a few weeks of current notes when something seemed strangely familiar with one of the new sermons. Confused, I looked through the stack of the prior year's sermons and froze. I double-checked. I couldn't believe it. He had recently repeated a few of the sermons from the year before. "You can do that?" I thought. I guessed there was some reason for it. He certainly would know what he was allowed to do. But why would he do that? Maybe it was a mistake. I didn't know what to think about it, so I decided to hand in the notes talk to him some other time.

After a few more weeks, it was time to hand in the sermon notes. To make sure I hadn't imagined it, I pulled out my old sermon notes to compare and was astonished again. Yep. They were the same. Three out of five sermons were duplicates of last year. What was going on here? Why was he doing this? Many questions ran through my mind. Several possible answers too. Maybe some sermons were required by the church, or maybe there was some special schedule known only to spiritual leaders that were especially sensitive to the needs of the people. Who knew?

I decided to keep with my original plan to ask about the sermons and then about Life Anew. This made sense because I was sure there was some logical explanation about the repeated sermons, and then we could delve into the more complex question I had about the two religions. I was leaning toward staying with the Lutheran church because it was bigger, older, and more stable, but I was still looking forward to hearing what he had to say about Life Anew.

Weeks passed. Time and time again, I lost my nerve to have the discussion with the pastor and get on with that part of my life. But how could I just walk up to him and start a conversation? On the other hand, he was the only one I knew could help me figure this out. I had to do it and do it soon.

It was a typical Sunday morning, and the service just ended. We were all in line, waiting to leave the sanctuary after greeting the pastor. I couldn't ask him such a weighty question while in line with everyone else. I had to gamble and see him in a few minutes after he changed to his suit and emerged from his office. Eventually, I saw him come into the narthex. It was perfect timing, not too many people around.

"Hello, Pastor," I said, freaking out on the inside.

"Good morning again, Scott," he said warmly. He was looking his usual authoritative self after leading the worship service, speaking the words of God from the pulpit, making everyone feel safe.

"I have a question, or actually two, that I was wondering if you could help me with," I said, stumbling over every word.

"Go ahead, what's on your mind?" He said with a smile as he looked down at me. He seemed ten feet tall.

"Well, the first question is a small one, and it has to do with the sermons. You see, I started taking notes last year, and I noticed that . . . some of the sermons were repeated this year and, and, and, and I was wondering why you did that?" I blurted with surprising clarity, sweat forming on my hands and forehead. This was good because it made me a little more comfortable to ask the real question I would ask after this one.

And then, the comment that changed my world and started me on a lifelong search. "Well Scott," the pastor said, then paused. A wave of surprise washed over his face. After a long moment, he placed his hand on my shoulder, leaned close to me, and whispered, "I'm sorry." Looking down sheepishly, he added, "It's a tough job."

Then silence.

THE AFTERMATH

The greatly anticipated, far-reaching, and definitive answer from the pastor was nowhere to be found. Not only that, his answer left me feeling that he might be over his head in his job. His job? He was supposed to be a spiritual leader and know things, a lot of important things. Could he be just like everybody else, struggling to get through the week? Even more disturbing, if he was struggling with writing sermons, how could he help me with the much weightier questions relating to Life Anew and the born-again version of Christianity? If the pastor couldn't help me, then who could?

Looking through the eyes of a developmental psychologist, the pressure I placed on myself to resolve these seemingly conflicting theological and religious constructs originated in my childhood. It could have stemmed from Mom's propensity for lists and organizational drive. Or perhaps it was Dad's authoritarian demeanor that created a need for me to view the world in an all-or-nothing perspective. Or maybe it was Glenn's influence in thinking for me and telling me what to do. Whatever the reasons, it was impossible for me to hold these competing concepts for more than a short while. I had to pick one. When my pastor revealed he might be struggling with his "job," my confidence in him eroded, and I felt alone with my questions.

    I had to find out for myself.

SLOW DELIBERATION

Months passed, and I was confirmed and going to the Bethlehem church whenever I could. Learning about this church was more compelling to me than the Lutheran church because the people were younger, livelier, and exhibited a realness about knowing God not seen in the Lutheran church. After the disappointing response from my pastor, I decided to throw myself into learning more about what this born-again thing was all about.

Not too long after spending time with the people at Bethlehem church, I learned that most of them had "accepted Christ" and therefore were born-again Christians or Evangelical Christians. The word "Evangelical" was in connection to preaching the born-again message and converting others to Christianity. The critical event of accepting Christ was controversial even within non-denominational groups. When a speaker was talking about becoming a Christian, they usually referred to a single point in time when a person "accepted" Christ and became a Christian. Typically, a person came to that point in their lives where they wanted to experience God in a new and more profound way. Another phrase used to explain this event was "inviting Jesus into your heart" or to "opening the door to Jesus." Another common term was to "have a personal relationship with Jesus." This was most intriguing to me since it spoke powerfully of the two-way interaction I was so curious about.

The single defining moment of accepting Christ did not happen to every born-again Christian. For individuals who didn't experience this, being a Christian was something they just grew up with. One or both of their parents were born-again Christians and, at a young age, someone asked them if they accepted Jesus, and they agreed. If they were too young to remember their decision, their parents told them that they committed their life to the Lord when they were younger. Sometimes these people developed doubts about their relationship with God after hearing about the importance of the single-point-in-time experience. When this topic came up in discussions and talks, it was always suggested to be sensitive to these people when talking about the conversion experience.

The entire concept was different from other religions I knew about because the emphasis was on knowing and having a relationship with God. It was the "knowing" part that had me baffled. The only thing about knowing Christ that I knew was that I didn't know if I knew Him. And how did one know for sure anyway? It wasn't that I didn't want to know. Sometimes people asked me, "Are you a Christian, Scott?"

"No, I don't think so," I replied sheepishly, wishing I knew what I could do to honestly answer in the affirmative and be embraced by the group. There was no doubt I was an outsider, and I wanted in.

As time passed, my desire to have what the others had; to know without a doubt, I was a Christian, grew exponentially. I wanted to experience the key moment of accepting Christ and at last, be welcomed as a Christian. Through listening to sermons, talks, and reading pamphlets on how to become a Christian, I discovered that accepting Christ was a four-part process. There are many variations, but most of them contained some combinations of the following parts:

1. Every person is born as a sinner, apart from God, and not a Christian.
2. People who are sinners cannot please God and are condemned to death.
3. God sent his son Jesus Christ to provide a way to pay for our sins and enable us to have a relationship with God and go to heaven when we die.
4. The way to be saved from this death sentence was to accept Jesus as the one true Savior and have faith that he will intervene on our behalf before God, removing our sins and enabling us to live with him in heaven.

Each of the parts had scripture references. The verses were included to show the Plan of Salvation was factual, as I saw with both the Bethlehem church people and the Life Anew group. They understood the Bible better than anyone I knew. They would spout off numerous verses, stories, and provide the book, chapter and verse to each of them, which always impressed me.

So, the way a person accepted Christ was to pray the "sinners' prayer." Jesus would come into your heart, and you were forgiven, a born-again Christian. You had the promise then, to live forever in Heaven. The prayer had a few variations but usually went something like this:

> "Dear Jesus, I know I'm a sinner, please forgive me and accept me into your kingdom. Amen."

When people conveyed their conversion experiences, they spoke about unfortunate life experiences and helplessness. Whether it was bad relationships, events outside of their lives, or the inability to conquer self-destructive behaviors, many shared that in their darkest hour, they turned to God. Subsequently, an external feeling of peace and contentment rushed into their heart and mind. Some even suggested they perceived Christ appearing or speaking directly to them with a message of love and acceptance. A feeling of helplessness was a common experience that drove people to accept Christ. The philosopher, Soren Kierkegaard's description of "coming to the end of yourself," was a good description, or the popularized version, "let go and let God." In either case, the idea was to stop trying to control your own life and relinquish control to God. I remember thinking that this seemed scary. What would happen if I recited that prayer? Would a spirit rush into my body? Would I be taken over by some other force? What would happen to "me?" To who I already was? I wasn't sure, and these questions churned in my mind.

CORNERED!

In the summer before my sophomore year in high school, the Bethlehem church youth group planned a retreat at a conference center a few hours away. Glenn was going too. Everyone was friendly enough, so I felt comfortable, except when the topic of becoming a Christian was raised. When I sensed the conversation heading in that direction, I had to duck out carefully.

The conference center was nestled among hundreds of acres of rolling fields interspersed with small stands of trees, and a winding stream. Several small, rustic cabins stood on the property, each containing bunk beds and with a small porch out front. They were centrally located to a large main building for eating and gathering. Not far from the main building was a large pond encircled by a well-worn walking path.

I found out before I signed up for the weekend that the purpose of the retreat was to have fun and learn about God through Bible studies and lectures. Our youth pastor, William, was especially excited about a particular guest lecturer. The van ride was fun as usual, listening to William and his antics. After we arrived, we picked cabins and were told to get settled and report to the main cabin for dinner. I had brought my collapsible fishing pole with me and was pleased to see the pond on the drive up the long gravel driveway to the center. I asked around and found out I could fish during the free time. I planned to get up early the next morning and try my luck.

I had been fishing for at least three or four seasons with my friends. I usually fished the first day of trout season, and then after school and Saturdays in local streams. The collapsible pole I had was fantastic. I could strap it to my bike and be on my way. I used a lure so I didn't have to dig up worms and figure out a way to carry the bait to their death sentence. My *Rapala* lure was identical to a small minnow, and when gently pulled through the water, it wriggled back and forth like a real fish. Attached to the front and back of it were two three-pronged barbed hooks designed to capture the unsuspecting fish efficiently.

My catch over the years was limited to sunfish and one or two catfish that were too small to eat. One time, on the first day of trout season, I actually caught a dead fish. It didn't put up much of a fight. Strangely enough, it was the biggest catch of the day. No one wanted to eat it. I threw it back for someone else to recatch.

At the retreat, I was up early the next morning and quietly got my gear and walked to the pond. It was warm in the sun, and the deep blue sky reflected in the pond. As usual, I caught nothing. Time after time, I flung my lure out as far as I could and slowly reeled in the fake fish lure. After about an hour or so I was getting hot and tired, so I started to head around the pond back to the cabins casting as I went. I was about to collapse my pole when I noticed two dark objects far from the shore. I looked again. Sure enough, they were two good-sized fish. I had no clue what they were, but they were big. My heart pounded, and I thought this could be the big catch of the day, or week, or year. Not wanting to miss the opportunity, I set up my rod and prepared to unleash the cast of my life. I had to launch it far enough past the two fish to not scare them off. One, two, three, make this a good one — a five-foot cast. The little minnow slammed into the water with great force. Crap. Try again, Dammit. Even shorter. Maybe I would have better luck if I swam out there with a rock and attempted to pummel them to death. Okay, relax. Try again, slowly, but with force. Finally, a perfect cast, fifteen feet past the two, and they didn't move. Heart pounding, excitement level raising, I pulled the minnow-bait back. I slowly pulled that little guy right between the two large black shapes. One darted off immediately, the other remained motionless then began to swim toward the lure. Should I pull it faster? Slower? I didn't know. I didn't usually catch fish when I fished. "Steady as she goes." Captain Kirk always told Chekov on the bridge of the Enterprise in times like these. So that's what I did.

In a split second the plastic minnow was engulfed entirely by one of the attackers. If the little fish was real, it wouldn't even know what hit him, but then if it was real, it wouldn't have swum between two giant fish right around breakfast time. It was hooked well. I reeled it in slowly. It didn't fight much, so I thought it was probably a catfish, not a trout. I almost caught many trout in my day, and they all had some tug and pull to them before they leaped off my line.

ANGEL IN TRAINING

As I was reeling in my prey, I realized I had no idea what I was going to do with it. I wanted to clean and cook him but didn't know how to do either. I had always fished with my friends, and they always assured me they would help if needed. But it was never needed. So, I figured I would just let this one go.

"Looks like you've got a big one." Came a deep voice from behind me.

Startled by the interruption, I said "Yup, it's a big one. Not much fight, though." I said, not recognizing who was coming.

"Are you going to eat it?" The voice offered as he emerged from the brush. It was the guest speaker for the weekend. William had introduced him in in the first session, and his name was John. He was middle-aged, not too tall, and slightly overweight. He had kind eyes and a gentle voice.

"Well, I tend to let most of them go," I lied, thinking he'd see me as some sort of animal rights activist and be impressed.

"I know how to clean and cook him if you want some help." Was I that transparent? Did he somehow know that I had no idea what I was doing? I didn't respond, pretending to be caught up in extracting this aquatic life-form from his world into ours.

"Actually, I don't have a lot of experience with this," I confessed, feeling awkward at the prospect of imposing on this person I just met.

"No problem at all," He replied, as he proceeded to help me haul in my catch. It was a large catfish, maybe 6 or 7 pounds with beautiful deep olive coloring and the characteristic whisker-like feelers called "barbels." He told me that he would take it into the kitchen, clean it so that we could split it for lunch.

I was elated, and it changed the weekend for me. I had a connection with the weekend guest speaker, and everyone would soon know, even William. Maybe John would mention our fishing rendezvous in a talk.

After breakfast, there were a few interactive sessions and lectures. As the morning progressed, people asked me how the fishing expedition went. I told them about my catch, and that John was preparing it for us for lunch. Each time I conveyed the story, people's eyebrows raised because I was friends with the guest speaker. At lunchtime, I didn't see John, so I joined the line to get my meal. Just then, John came out from the kitchen with a plate of corn-breaded filet of catfish. The fish was excellent, and I basked in the attention that came along with the meal.

In the talk after dinner that night, John was explaining the historical and political context of the life of Jesus, when he mentioned he would lead us all in a communion service at the end of his lecture. That sounded nice. I was used to receiving communion at my Lutheran church. What jolted me was when he threw in a qualifier, "The communion service is open to all that have accepted Jesus into your heart and have been born-again with Christ."

Oh, that's just great. Talk about feeling trapped. I knew I didn't have a born-again experience; everyone probably thought I was a Christian. I couldn't lie, but I couldn't tell the truth. What should I do? Could I fake an illness, or just not show up? Oh, this was not good. My newfound friend John would start wondering what was up with me. Maybe he would find out I wasn't a Christian. Maybe he would think that I used him to cook my fish. This was not good, not good at all. I obsessed.

After much internal deliberation, I nobly decided to throw all decency aside and go through with the communion. I was confirmed as a Lutheran, so I guessed there was nothing wrong with that. The whole thing was between God and me anyway, and there were far worse things I could have done.

After dinner, John began with his talk. He was an excellent speaker and knew how to state ideas clearly. I don't recall every detail, but he connected stories from the New and Old Testaments together with present-day applications. He had a soft and authoritative voice and a sincere gaze that was captivating. At the end of the talk, he announced that we would participate in a communion service. Gulp. Paper plates piled with torn pieces of bread and plastic cups of grape juice were placed on a long table in the front of the room. Then he went into a recounting of the Last Supper, the story every one of us had heard many times before, but this time with his masterful presentation skills.

After this moving account, John motioned to a few people to distribute the bread. He told us to wait until he instructed us to eat the bread. As the plates of bread were being passed out, he spoke about how vital communion was to those who believed in Jesus. And then he said the words that caused my stomach to churn.

"May anyone who eats of this bread who has not accepted Jesus, choke on the body of Christ until they accept Him as their Lord and Savior," proclaimed John, in a deep, commanding voice. Now, what should I do? I had a piece of bread in my hand. Should I put it back? Hide it and throw it away later? Did I dare eat it and risk the bread supernaturally changing in my mouth to some bitter-tasting substance? Would I then fall to the floor in front of the group, choking and vomiting bile and proving to everyone that I wasn't a Christian? What to do, what to do, what to do!

Reluctantly, I went for it. I slowly - very slowly - chewed the bread. It was just bread, a symbol, just bread. God was not some grim reaper or angel of death gunning for me. Or at least I hoped not. I chewed the bread so finely there was no way to choke. Nothing happened. Thank God.

I passed on the juice. I had already pressed my luck too far.

LOOKING FOR THAT BORN AGAIN FEELING

The retreat was the last straw. The pressure of feeling like an outsider was too much to bear. One night, back in my room at home, I decided to recite the prayer. I didn't know what was going to happen. Would a light appear? Would I see a vision, or hear a voice? I didn't know; no one ever explained what to expect. I was upset because I wanted to put the religion dilemma behind me and be able to tell people that I really was a Christian, a born-again Christian. So, I prayed, "Dear Jesus, I know I'm a sinner, please forgive me and accept me into your kingdom. Amen."

Nothing happened.
So, I said it again.
Nothing.
And again.
Still nothing. Then I fell asleep.

For the next several weeks I was frequently praying the prayer whenever I felt the need. No voices, visions, or mystical experiences. This was starting to remind me of fishing; lots of effort, no results. I was growing tense, anxious, and frustrated. It was as if I was looking at an inviting pool of water, but unable to dive in. Or, in one of those dreams where you are trying to run but can't.

Then, something happened.

I was lying in bed, thinking about my spiritual crisis. Over and over, faster and faster, my thoughts churned. My parents were in their room across the hall, getting ready for bed. Dad, as usual, was humming fragments of familiar tunes. All the while, my anxiety continued to grow to a fever pitch. I had been thinking and praying long enough, ducking questions about my born-again status.

The room was dark; I was alone and exceedingly upset. I began to cry silently. Then, an odd sensation washed over me; a wave of warmth and peace immediately relaxed me. I hadn't recently prayed the sinner's prayer, but the sensation came anyway. I had a feeling that God was there in the room with me. It wasn't a vision, voice, light, or angel. Nothing concrete came to me, just these feelings of peace and connectedness with something much bigger than me. God, or heaven, or something. I wasn't sure what it was. I just took it all in for a while.

Finally, I thought this was something tangible and real. I guessed this was what everyone was talking about with that moment in time, interaction or real experience with God. I would claim this as "The Moment," the point in time. I could say from then on that I was a born-again Christian.

ANGEL IN TRAINING

The next day, I awoke and recalled the experience from the night before. I felt relieved, but not much different. I didn't have any special insights; no verses came to mind. I checked the mirror, and I looked the same. I had heard about this at church. People said that adopting Christianity didn't mean your life would profoundly change or become perfect. You would still have bad days and frustrations just as you had before Jesus entered your life. But the difference now was that God was with you, and you were not alone. More importantly, for me, I felt I could be a real part of the Christian group, no longer an outsider. Finally.

I went to school and cross-country practice as usual, with no incident. No one came up to me saying they saw me glowing. I wasn't going to blab about it either. I was shy, and it wasn't like I was going to change now. I didn't even share it with the Bethlehem group for months. It only came up when someone asked me if I was a Christian and I confidently said yes. Communion was received with no fear of choking. It felt good to belong. But now I had a new problem.

My new dilemma was that I wanted my friends and family to experience and know what I had come to accept as the "Truth." At the Bethlehem church, we were encouraged to preach the gospel. Just as Jesus and his disciples traveled from town to town, so should we spread the gospel. The word "gospel" means "good news" and refers to salvation through Jesus. If anyone did not accept Jesus as their Lord and Savior, they were going to suffer for eternity in hell. People needed a way to escape this fate and be united with God, just like I was. We were taught there was no other way to get to God except through Christianity, and we were shown verse after verse that backed that up. The main one was the famous John 3:16

> "For God so loved the world that he gave his one and only Son, that whoever believes in him shall not perish but have eternal life."

Christianity made the most sense to me out of all the religions I knew. I learned that we were born in sin because Adam and Eve ate of the tree of good and evil in the Garden of Eden. God made everything, and they could have or do anything except for eating from the tree. But they ate from the tree anyway, and when God found out he kicked them out of the Garden, and all of humanity was cursed to die apart from Him. But God, out of his compassion for us, provided a way to get back to him. This was promised to Abraham, who was the first of the Hebrew race or the Jews. The Savior Jesus, who was a Jew, took away the sins of the world, setting us free. This gift of salvation was available to anyone that accepted Jesus as their "Lord and Savior." If you didn't believe in Him, then you would be condemning *yourself* to eternal damnation.

Why wouldn't everyone want to have their sins forgiven and "know" they would be in heaven when they died? Wouldn't everyone come to the same conclusion as I did and accept Christ? I understood that I initially struggled with the decision, but it was crystal clear for me now, and they needed to know the "Truth."

Throughout the next two years, as I entered my senior year of high school, I embraced the realization that

Christianity was the only religion that dealt completely with the issue of sin. Although I had nagging doubts about the origin of sin in the Garden of Eden, I wholeheartedly embraced the salvation message as valid. It felt right; it was right. And since it was right, others had to know about it. What if they went throughout their lives not knowing this message? Truly this was a fate worse than death.

In the meetings and Bible studies I attended, the question frequently surfaced about others we knew who "did not know Jesus" and the best way we could talk to them. Many times, the leaders encouraged us to pray for the right time to talk to them. Now and then, someone shared how, after much time praying for a dear friend or family member, they received a call from them saying they found Jesus and dedicated their life to Christ. Their friends were forever grateful that they cared enough to talk to them and pray that they would become Christians.

Two people on my mind were two of my best friends, Alan and Tom. I had to talk to them. The question was when.

SWING AND A MISS

Alan and Tom were my buddies. I was especially close to Alan since he lived closer to me. We were all on the wrestling team, and being such an intense sport, it tends to create deep friendships. I spent considerable time at Alan's house and him at mine. I knew Alan was Catholic, but I didn't think he went to church all the time, and I wasn't sure about Tom, but I thought he was Episcopalian.

We spent a lot of time together at school and playing sports. For a long time, I didn't even think about mentioning the subject of Christianity with them. They knew I went to a different church from the Lutheran church where I was confirmed, but no one questioned it. One day I was asked during a Bible study at Bethlehem Church about who I planned to pray about to become a Christian, Alan and Tom immediately came to mind. So, that's what I did. At meetings and home, I prayed that I would be able to share the Gospel with them.

Many Evangelical Christian churches hosted events offering programs of general appeal coupled with a presentation of the Gospel. Many times, sports figures were used to draw an audience where the player talked about their star-struck life and about how they came to know Jesus and how important it was to them.

Usually, at these events, there was an alter call inviting all who did not know Jesus to make a public profession of their decision to become a Christian. The public announcement was stressed many times as part of the conversion process, to demonstrate who was serious about their decision. When Bethlehem Church group announced their plans to hold an event, I was excited.

They organized an evening with a world-class strong man. He had begun as a champion weight lifter, and then went on the road conducting superhuman feats and sharing the Gospel. I invited Alan to come with me. The strong man was impressive. He pressed a 250-pound dumbbell with one hand. He also asked several people to sit on a table, and he went under it and lifted it off the floor by pressing up with his back. It was truly amazing.

After the physical demonstration, he told us about his life of hardship, how he wandered from place to place with no direction, living life as a "loser." Then someone introduced him to Jesus, and he turned his life over to him. Now his life had a purpose, and he knew that he would spend eternal life with God living now as a "winner." He was a charismatic speaker and presented a moving account of his life and how God had helped him in his greatest hour of need. He ended with an emotional crescendo and an invitation to accept Jesus. This man obviously felt deeply about his message. Alan and I didn't speak about the message after the show. I didn't know what to say, so I let it go.

As the months went by, I was praying and thinking about how and when I could mention my Christian experience with Alan or Tom, but nothing came to me. They had to know the Truth; they had to learn what I experienced. Then it happened. One evening the three of us were hanging out at Tom's house talking about teachers, wrestling, and school, and probably girls. At some point, I blurted out, "Hey, you know what? If we all happened to die tonight, I would be the only one to go to heaven."

I knew it was blunt. But it was the truth, and I wanted them to know.

Their faces conveyed all their feelings. Tom was shocked, wide-eyed and mouth open; it was as if he was hit with a 2x4. Alan drew back with arms crossed as if he shut down. They both had several questions about why I said what I said, and where I got this information. I responded by logically mapping out the sin and salvation message just as I had worked through the concept with the Bethlehem church group. They weren't initially angry. All of us were seniors in high school and had known each other since elementary school. Our friendship was strong, and at first, despite their initial reactions, they took in every word I said. I did my best to tell them what I knew; that every person was born into sin and that going to church wasn't enough. They had to know Jesus and accept him into their heart in order to be saved. The good news was that there was a way to be saved. The bad news was that I wasn't sure what exactly they should do. Should they pray the sinner's prayer? Shouldn't a religious leader do it, a minister, pastor, or priest? I was angry at myself for not knowing what to do. I waited all this time to talk to them, and I wasn't as prepared as I wanted to be.

Then it came to me. Glenn would know exactly what to do. Yes! I would call him, and he could come over and fix this. I asked to use the phone and called home. Darn it! He wasn't home. I went back in and said that they had to wait until tomorrow.

One of them said, "So, what if we die tonight? What is going to happen then?" I told them I didn't know, but that I didn't think that God was that much of a nitpicker. They appeared to accept that, but we still ended the evening on a very uncomfortable note.

The next night, they came over, and Glenn showed them some of the brochures about the Christian message. They didn't have the reaction I expected. They seemed less interested than the night before, and I sensed Tom was a little edgy. He asked questions like, "Where did these brochures come from?" and "What church put out these materials?" He kept a distance from us and was not his familiar warm and friendly self. Maybe he spoke to his parents or a priest? Perhaps he thought I was introducing them to a cult.

This evening ended with less emotional intensity than the night before. I felt better because they had the brochures with them that explained the salvation message and, importantly, the method to obtain salvation, including the text of the sinner's prayer. It felt like our friendships were back on track. At least that's what I thought was happening.

Not too long after that evening, I spoke with Alan about what happened. To my dismay, he said he felt more comfortable with his Catholic religion. He also told me that Catholicism was a Christian religion too, and they probably weren't all that different. When he said that, something welled up inside me, an intense frustration, a desire, even anger. I wanted to grab and shake him to understand. No, it wasn't the same. It was different; it was real, not some stuffy religion. Most importantly, it made sense, it was right, the only correct religion, the only true way to God. I forgot about the times of doubting I worked through and was overtaken by the frustration of how he could not accept what I had presented.

Despite my internal dialogue and feelings, I didn't know what else to say, so I let it go. I figured Alan would have to learn the truth some other way, some other time. Tom, on the other hand, had a different reaction.

Apparently, sometime after the two evenings of explaining the Gospel, Tom spoke to his mom and someone at his church. He and his mother's reaction to the Gospel ranged between anger and contempt. I had a brief conversation with both Tom and his mom, and it centered on how I could tell someone they were going to hell. They told me this was just my opinion, and who did I think I was telling people who was and who wasn't going to heaven? I tried to explain that it wasn't my idea, but God's message contained in the Bible. It wasn't my idea that if people don't accept Christ, they will burn in hell. God said it in the Bible. That response has helped me many times when arguing about Christian beliefs with my friends because it diverted the judgment from me to God.

My friendship with Tom at that point was nonexistent. Sometimes, high school friendships grow apart as different interests develop. But this was different. It was sudden and severe. Making things even worse, another event created even more of a strain on my relationship with Tom.

ANGEL IN TRAINING

I was out driving around with another friend, Chris, on a Friday night in the fall of our senior year with nothing to do. I think I wanted to break the ice with Tom, or, most likely, not thinking at all when we decided to pull a prank on Tom. I heard about it but never had the opportunity to pull off a caper like this. We would get two cinderblocks, bring them to his house, jack up the back of his car, remove the wheels, and set the car on the blocks. This would be great. We knew he had his own car and guessed with his parents having two, his car would be parked in the driveway. We knew where he lived and I had the cinderblocks, so off we went.

Chris and I arrived at Tom's house at 1:00 AM and quietly used the lug wrench and jack from my car to carefully remove the two rear wheels from Tom's car, one at a time, and replaced them with the blocks. It was perfect; the back of the car was only slightly higher than with the wheels on. We stacked the two wheels just around the corner of the garage and placed all the lug nuts on the top wheel so they could be easily seen. We could have been jerks and hidden the lug nuts and wheels, but this was a prank, it would be funny. Well, that was the intention.

The next day, my partner in crime and I met up at our school's home football game. We were sitting in the stands watching the game and reminiscing about our prank when we saw a few other friends walking by and waved to them to join us. As they came closer, we saw they had concerned looks on their faces. That was strange because we were clearly winning the football game and nothing of note was happing on the field.

"Did you hear what happen at the soccer game this morning?" One of them asked.

"What happened," I replied, "did someone get hurt?"

"No." One of them replied. "Someone jacked-up Tom's car, he missed the bus to the game and, because of that, they lost."

Oh . . . my . . . God. We learned later that Tom, who was captain of the team, had overslept and went rushing out to his car, jumped in, put the car in reverse. The engine raced, but the car didn't go anywhere. He got out and saw that his car was inoperable. Looking around, he didn't see the wheels, so he ran back into the house to get the keys to one of his parents' cars. A good idea except that his car was parked diagonally in front of both garage doors, blocking both vehicles. A detail we missed as we were executing our nefarious plan. By the time he and his parents found the wheels and replaced them, Tom missed the bus driving the soccer team from our school to the away game. And, by the time he found directions to the school and arrived, he was not able to play until an official break later in the game. He was a strong player, so the loss could very well have been the result of him not playing the whole game.

Apparently, this was a big game, and all the players were upset. To this day, I have no idea how, but Tom found out that Chris and I were the culprits. I saw him in the hallway at school a few days later. With a look as cold as steel, he said, "Nice, Scott, nice."

"I'm sor..." I tried to convey, but he disappeared down the crowded hall. I felt terrible.

After high school, Alan and Tom remained friends, but I did not see or talk with Tom at all. I occasionally asked Alan how Tom was feeling about the whole thing, and he told me Tom was still pretty upset, especially about the "going to hell" thing.

The next time I saw Tom was at our tenth high school reunion. Reunions were always a mixture of emotions, regrets, and positive memories. I wondered if Tom would be there and how he was doing. I also looked forward to seeing other schoolmates.

I entered the banquet hall and scanned the crowd when I saw Tom. He was sitting at a round table of about eight people, his back to me. When others at the table saw me, they called out my name, asking me to join them. This got Tom's attention, and he turned around.

"Do you still think I'm going to hell?" he snapped, glowering from his seat.

Caught off guard by his anger, I mumbled something incoherent. "Well, I ... no . . . er . . . so what have you been up to?" This lame attempt to change the subject seemed to work, and we continued an awkward conversation for a few minutes. My mind was racing while talking to him and trying to adjust to his reaction. With a sneer on his face, he told me that he had attended medical school and had become a doctor. Not sure if others heard his initial salvo, I scanned the table. Thankfully, it appeared either no one else had heard him, or they didn't understand what he was talking about. The group continued their respective conversations. I was amazed because it seemed as if no time had passed since high school. How could someone hang on to their anger for so long? I was puzzled and saddened that a handful of statements could so easily erase all the good times we had over the years.

Many questions came to mind. Why could Alan get over it and not Tom? Could I have said things differently? Maybe

I screwed up by saying what I said, but at the same, time, I only had good intentions. How could I not have told the truth? I had learned from church that sometimes people were persecuted because they were Christians and jailed for preaching the Gospel. Maybe this was my first experience with religious rejection. I wasn't sure, but I couldn't change my beliefs. I felt justified but still was bothered by how poorly my message of salvation was received.

Side note – Fast forward 30 years – In October 2015, the high school wrestling team Tom and I were on in 1974 was being inducted into the high school's hall of fame. The wrestlers and their friends and families were invited to the celebration. It was a wonderful time connecting with many old friends and reminiscing about that tremendous year. I hadn't seen Tom in the 30 years since our altercation at our tenth reunion and was looking for him throughout the evening. So far, so good. But at the end of the evening, we were all standing in a large reception area when I looked across the room and saw Tom, who instantly caught my eye.

I screamed in my head as he started walking in my direction. With my blood pressure rising and with nowhere to go, the only escape was to sprint out the door. Since I couldn't do that, I had no other choice but to meet him head-on. To my surprise, as he came closer, he was smiling.

"Hi Scott, how have you been? It's been some time," he said, giving me a hardy handshake.

"Fine, Tom, and how have you been?" I said, thinking *God take me now*.

"You know, Scott, we had a conversation back in high school that threw me off," he said, eyes fixed directly on mine.

Crap, here it comes, wave two of the retribution tour. I thought.

Tom continued, "You told me I wasn't a Christian, even though I thought I was. I mean, I went to church and all that. You caused me to think about what I was doing, and I questioned my faith. After many years of searching, I came to know the Lord and am now a Christian and very happy. I just wanted to thank you."

Quite shocked that I didn't get another verbal lashing, the only thing I could muster was, "Wow. Well, you're welcome. Good luck with that."

Little did he know, I was in quite a different place in my spiritual journey.

PRAYER FROM A DIFFERENT PLACE

Prayer has been a consistent topic of investigation for me, starting with the scripted bedtime prayers and asking the blessing before dinner. In high school, when I was adapting to my new-found relationship with God, prayer was now a whole different ballgame. Before becoming a Christian, all I could hope for was a glorified Christmas list - now I had an inside track. I was in and had direct access to God. I was like an Old Testament high priest; I could go into the holy of holies. Now I could be in the presence of God any time I wanted. If I had any doubts, I could remember that night when I felt a special connection with God. I knew I was a Christian and had special admission to God. This experience, together with the Bible verses I learned, confirmed I was "one with Christ." I was forgiven and going to heaven.

Even though I was a Christian, many of my prayers during these years were colored with anxiety, reflecting my ongoing insecurities. I spent many hours in prayer, asking for guidance, direction, and help with anxiety about many things. As a result, my prayers were looking for an outcome from God. I hoped that my pleadings would be heard, and God would move to help me win a wrestling match, to figure out where I was going to college, and how to get through each day. I thought about the relationship with God. I heard so much about when people spoke about walking with and talking with Jesus and having a friend in Jesus. I wanted something tangible to happen, a voice, a sign, a conversation. That never happened. The comfort I received came more from knowing that I did everything possible to plead my case, and the rest was up to God. I believed he heard me and would do whatever was according to his will. I heard a saying during these years that had stuck with me. God has three answers to prayer. Yes, no, and wait. For me, the toughest answer was "wait."

The first big test of prayer and my faith came when I was deciding where to go to college. I talked to everyone about my options. I prayed about it, and thought about it, and talked some more, but nothing specific came through. I had a keen interest in graphic arts and photography, so that provided some direction. Another possible path came from wrestling. I was pretty good at it, and Glenn was enjoying his time wrestling at a conservative Evangelical Christian college in the Midwest, was even the big man on campus. I visited the school a few times and got a feel of the atmosphere. The good part was that everyone there was Christian and a lot of fun. All students were required to attend Chapel from time to time, where I assumed a church-type service took place.

The tone of this school was light, not somber or overly religious. It was refreshing. One time, when Glenn and I were walking past a dormitory, a booming voice blasted from one of the windows. The thundering voice proclaimed the arrival of the star wrestler, my brother. The funny part was that this announcer's voice was a spot-on replication of Billy Graham, the well-known evangelist. Glenn told me the first time anyone heard this impersonation was during a chapel service where this student was scheduled to present a short sermon. The reaction wavered between shock and waiting for lightning to strike, to waves of mumbled laughter.

While that was all comfortable, something seemed odd to me. Here were a few thousand students, all proclaiming to be Evangelical Christians, studying at an undergraduate school with an all-Evangelical Christian faculty. I guessed it was good to get a Christian view of history, theology, and religion; but what about math and science? Were there Christian perspectives on them as well? As I thought more about this, I began to wonder if this was a good thing or not. The environment seemed too homogeneous. Everyone believed the same thing, with no opposing views. Now I was torn.

Late in the winter of 1975, during my senior year of high school, the decision about my future loomed. I felt my relationship with God had to work; that was what the born-again Christian movement was all about after all. To me, having a special relationship with God was the central element in being a Christian. I felt relieved being able to converse with God about everything and getting answers to prayer. Nevertheless, I was wondering about the all-Christian school concept, struggling with my vocational interests, and wrestling in the New Jersey state finals all at the same time when I came up with one way to make the decision. I prayed that if I placed 3rd or higher in the finals, I would go to my brother's school. This seemed the most expedient way for God to give me an answer. Deep down, I didn't love wrestling, but maybe I should use what talent I had for God's glory in a Christian school.

As it turned out, I lost in the quarter-finals. I was done with wrestling and was surprised by how relieved I felt. I knew then that going to school with my brother would not have been good for me. I wondered if it was God that answered my prayers, or if I had acted for what I wanted. I wasn't sure. What I did know was that the only subjects I had any interest in at all were graphic arts and photography, so I went to school for photography.

I chose the Rochester Institute of Technology (RIT) in New York. It was touted as one of the best schools for both commercial printing and photography in the country. My mom, concerned that I was going to a secular school, called the Student Affairs office to see if there were any Christian organizations on campus. She received information about several groups on campus, affiliated with many denominations. One group stood out from the others as being interdenominational and Christian-based. That caught her attention. The organization was called the Intervarsity Christian Fellowship (IV) with chapters on many college campuses throughout the US and Europe. It wasn't a church or associated with any specific theological beliefs. The group organized on-campus Bible studies, worship, and fellowship opportunities. Mom and I talked about meeting with one of the student leaders when we visited the school. At that time, I had no strong feelings one way or another about the group. I was too busy freaking out about going to a school where I didn't know a single person.

The tour went well, and I was impressed with the facilities. We got a chance to meet with Dan, the student president of the Intervarsity Christian Fellowship chapter at RIT. He was a nice enough fellow and told us a lot about the school and campus life. It turned out that Dan needed a roommate in the fall, and he asked if I was interested in rooming with him. With no other options in sight, I agreed.

After that, I felt better about starting school because, for the first time in my life, I was leaving home and going to live in a place where I didn't know anyone.

Good or bad, right or wrong, answer to prayer or not . . . off I went.

THE IN CROWD

The years at RIT were academic as expected with any undergrad school setting. However, an unexpected education came through my involvement with the Intervarsity group (IV). The IV organization is considered a para-church group with no affiliations to any specific denomination or church. They are Evangelical Christian in their beliefs and have a propensity to be quite scholarly in many of their publications, events, and programs. I liked the group, especially at that time in my life, because I wanted to continue to learn about God. The activities sponsored by the IV organization differed from campus to campus, depending on what the local chapter chose to do. A student leadership group ran each chapter with an outside regional coordinator assigned to assist in running the branch. The regional coordinator met regularly with the student leaders to help build leadership skills, provide counseling in their personal spiritual growth, and conduct Bible studies. The coordinators were comparable to missionaries because they had to raise the bulk of their living expenses from private sources with the national IV organization contributing only a small amount.

Our chapter had a large group meeting once a week in addition to small group Bible studies throughout the week in member's dorm rooms. The large group meeting ranged from 25-40 students, and the small groups were usually 3 to 5 people. The general thrust of the group was Bible study, worship, and fellowship. Fellowship means hanging out with friends. Worship was singing old hymns and new songs usually lead by someone who could play the guitar. We had a bound copy of around 50 song lyrics, some containing guitar chords.

The IV organization provided a lot of instruction on how to study the Bible. Their primary approach was *inductive* Bible study and could take place in either the large group meeting, the small groups, or individually. The inductive method directs a person to read and glean meaning from a verse or passage. For example, in the passage where Jesus turned water into wine, an inductive study guide offered questions asking, "What was going on that day? Who was in attendance? Why were they there?" or "What did Jesus say to Mary? What did he say to the crowd?" Questions like this direct the reader to center on the passage itself. The interesting thing about this approach is that you didn't need any special background to be able to participate or learn something new. Through these studies, not only did we spend a lot of time reading and studying the Bible, but it also helped develop observational skills. The group provided opportunities for many theological discussions on all kinds of topics. Some focused on core beliefs like sin, salvation, and what Jesus did for us. Others were more general, relating to the nature of God, man, or how the relationship between us changed after "The Fall" when Adam ate the apple.

ANGEL IN TRAINING

Other topics I loved to learn about I called "side-line" subjects. They related to aspects of the Christian faith that were not central to basic tenets, at least in my opinion. Even though they weren't as basic as whether Jesus really rose from the dead or if there was actually a person named Moses, they were hot items of discussion for some Christians. Popular Evangelical Christian theologians wrote books and articles outlining their perspectives and supplying backup scripture and cultural background. Other Evangelical scholars opposing the ideas published rebuttal articles and books presenting their viewpoints. Some of these disagreements could get heated, to the extent of splitting churches and denominations. These intra-Christian ideological differences continue to sow division even today on topics such as homosexuality, women leadership, rock and roll music, television programming, and public education, to name a few.

In my undergrad years, one hotly contested topic was the reliability and infallibility of the Bible. This related to the idea that the Bible is absolutely true, containing no errors, and should be believed without question. This concept obviously draws a deep line in the sand by dismissing all the other religions, traditions, and cultures that are not based on the Judeo-Christian documents contained in the Bible. At the same time, the idea of the Bible being infallible provided security to those of us who needed to know for sure that what we believed was true and right. For me, at that time, it was a no-brainer. If God was powerful enough to make everything, then he could work it so that His message could be delivered in print for the world to understand. In my mind, it had to be that way, because, without this belief, the world would be in chaos with no hope of ever knowing the truth.

    Learning about the reasons why the Bible was a reliable document lead me through a forest of concepts, some more challenging than others. For example, the New Testament was not written down until at least 70 years after the death of Christ. A popular response to this was that the oral tradition at that time was so accurate, we could be assured the message was flawless. Passing historical information from generation to generation was done orally for several thousand years before the proliferation of written language. This was because most people could not read or afford materials on which to write. Proof of the reliability of the oral tradition came in 1948 with the discovery of the Dead Sea Scrolls containing most of the Old Testament books, along with some New Testament texts. These scrolls were hidden in a cave during the dispersion of Christians after the death of Christ to avoid being destroyed by the Roman authorities. When comparing them to current translations, there were few differences.

    In addition to answering the question of how the words of the Bible were able to survive centuries uncontaminated, the next issue was where the words originated. Many critics of our beliefs often said that men wrote the Bible, and therefore, it was subject to their interpretation and beliefs. This was a tough topic. We were told God inspired the various authors to write the Word of God down exactly as He meant it to be written. Some said God put his hand on the hand of the writer as it was being written. Many texts made supported the idea that the Bible was the Word of God and reliable, called "proof texts." Even though the texts were not an iron-clad argument, it was enough proof for me to defend and promote my faith. To me, the Bible was accurate, reliable, and The True Word of God.

This subject came up often when talking to people about what it meant to be a Christian. They said things like, "It seems like a narrow way of thinking, to just write off all other religions."

My answer would always be, "It's not something I made up. It's God's word as contained in the Bible that says these things."

I had a range of reactions to that from, "Oh, I never looked at it that way," to, "I understand what you are saying, but still will keep to my religion," to even, "No matter what you say, I don't believe God is that cruel."

Even though the reliability of the Bible was an important issue, there was a time when I began to back off the "totally without error" message. I read a few books written by Christian scholars addressing what they called the seemingly inaccurate statements corresponding to the two conflicting accounts of creation contained in the book of Genesis. For example, in the first chapter of Genesis, creation takes place over six days, and humankind was created after plants and animals. In the second chapter, creation is created in one day with man created first, then plants and animals, then woman. There are differing accounts of events in the New Testament as well. For example, the recounting of Christ's resurrection differs across the four Gospels. These are the four New Testament books, Matthew, Mark, Luke, and John. When comparing each account, discrepancies can be found in who initially went to the tomb, was the stone rolled away or not, what the disciples saw when they arrived, and what were they told to do — critics of the Bible jump on these discrepancies as proof that the Bible is inaccurate. Supporters of the Bible provide explanations in an attempt to reconcile the differences. After reviewing many of the explanations, I felt like some were a stretch, while others were plausible. Either way, it didn't shake me to the core. I was comfortable believing the Bible was a document containing the Truth. That was the core issue.

During my years at RIT participating in the IV fellowship, I gained broad exposure to many historical and theological aspects of Christianity, including:

- The debate between creation and evolution
- Beliefs about the morality of homosexuality
- Whether to talk about Santa Claus
- If a person could lose their salvation after being saved
- The immaculate conception
- What hell was like
- The nature of angels, demons, and Satan
- The lives of the Old Testament prophets and the New Testament disciples
- What the future would be like according to the Old Testament prophecies in the book of Daniel and the New Testament book of Revelation.
- My favorite question: If God is all-powerful, is he able to make a rock so big that even he can't lift it?

X GOES TO SEMINARY

While I was attending RIT, X had decided to head full time into the ministry. During his undergrad years, X attended the King's College in Briarcliff Manor, New York. This was a non-denominational liberal arts college that followed Evangelical Christian perspectives. Upon graduation, he announced that he wanted to go for his Master of Divinity degree and possibly become a minister. He had been accepted at Gordon Conwell Theological Seminary in Massachusetts, which also followed the conservative Evangelical Christian traditions. I was so proud of him. He was such a huge pillar in my life, so strong, quiet, a popular athlete, and most importantly, a devoted Christian. He took everything in his life seriously, and his faith was no exception. I knew he would be a great minister. Before he extricated himself from us, he and I had a strong connection. Many times, when we exchanged letters, he concluded with, "Your brother twice," referring to our spiritual connection.

CONFRONTATION

After a few years of regular involvement at the RIT chapter of the IV group, I became part of the student leadership or executive committee. We called it "exec" for short. It was rewarding to be part of thinking up activities, studies, and programs for the group. I felt honored to be a part of other's spiritual growth, encouraging them, offering answers to the challenges to our faith, and creating opportunities to share the Gospel with others.

One such opportunity came when I received a call from Eric, an elder from a local church. He sounded young, energetic, and personable. The church had set a goal to conduct an Evangelical outreach event on the RIT campus during the year and was wondering if we wanted to be a part of the organization and promotion. When I mentioned this to the others, we decided to talk with the church leaders to learn more, so I set the meeting.

We met at one of the open meeting rooms on the dorm side of RIT. There were four of us and four of them. The representatives of the church introduced themselves as elders of the small but rapidly growing church not two miles from campus. They told us that the church members had been praying for an opportunity to do some outreach on the campus because the sinful and secular environment of the school was endangering the lives of many students. My mind flashed to some of my dorm mates, classmates, and friends that were probably not Christians, but were good people and close friends. I felt an initial adverse reaction to his statement, and I wanted to tell him it wasn't as bad as he portrayed. It wasn't a Sodom and Gomorrah, and these were regular people. But what was I to say, these men were elders of a church, they were serious about what they believed God wanted them to do. I didn't want to be the one with the least amount of faith in the meeting.

The elders told us they had secured a commitment from a nationally recognized magician who had agreed to come to the Rochester area to perform. Not only that, the magician was a Christian who was committed to spreading the Gospel to campuses similar to RIT and would do the show for free if we set it up. This was exciting. We could sponsor an event that would appeal to everyone, mention our group, and even place material on a table at the back of the room for those who might be interested. It was perfect . . . until the elders continued.

Apparently, these serious-minded and committed elders had another approach to spreading the Gospel. One crucial factor, they continued, was the surprise factor. They wanted the magician to be a draw to people who otherwise would not seek out the Gospel message. None of the posters, flyers, or any other communication about the event could have mention of a religious message or the IV group because it might "tip-off" the prospective audience. When everyone was in the auditorium and about halfway through the show, the magician would address the audience and tell them about the most important thing in his life, his relationship with Jesus Christ. He would tell his life story of how he found life and peace in accepting Jesus as his personal savior and then invite anyone in the audience to come down to the stage and make a public profession that they had accepted Jesus and were now Christians. The elders and a few of us from the IV group would be there to help people to the front, pass out information, and answer any questions.

The covert part of the plan caught us off guard but didn't dampen our spirits, at least not yet. We concluded our meeting and promised to contact the elders shortly.

As the days passed, and the more I thought about it, my hesitations grew. I kept thinking of some of the guys in my dorm. How would they react as they sat through the show and then were ambushed by the Christian message? I wouldn't appreciate it if I were them. I brought up my concerns at the next IV student leaders meeting. Although one or two of the members didn't think it was that bad of an idea, I conveyed my feelings about it, and one of the other members agreed. After some discussion, we all decided that we did not want to be a part of the event the way the elders presented it. The next step was to determine who was going to talk to the elders and let them know our concerns. As I was outlining how the call should go, I realized I was doing all the talking, and all eyes were on me — a bad sign.

As I feared, I was the most logical person to make the call, which made me extremely uncomfortable. These were, after all, elders of a church. They were older, they were serious, and knew what they wanted. I was just a student.

Reluctantly, I called Eric and told him about our concerns. He was not happy. His serious but cordial behavior flashed impatience. Even though I suspected some resistance, I thought that he would understand to some extent. I recoiled at his impatient tone.

"You don't want to what?" Eric said in an abrupt and deep voice that raised in volume as he spoke.

"We, uh, don't . . . feel comfortable, uh, taking the audience by surprise with a Gospel message, sir," I replied, feebly, but effectively.

Lowering his volume slightly, but just as intense, and adding my name for effect he replied, "Look, Scott, we've been doing this for a long time, and it works with people. The audience will be much smaller if they think it's a Christian event."

"I understand, but, uh, but these are our friends, not just people. They trust us." I surprised myself with this response, but it was a good comeback. And it was the truth.

He tried to convince me to reconsider, but even though I was nervous, I could not let the show go as they wanted. The call ended shortly after it started with Eric saying he would confer with the others and call me in a few days. I felt relieved and immediately let the IV executive committee know what happened. It felt good to hear their reassuring voices. Eric called the next day and, to my surprise, asked if we would be amenable to adding a phrase on the posters and flyers for the event indicating "A Christian message will be presented during the presentation." We agreed, and the show was on.

The event went well. There was a good turnout. All communications indicated that the IV group sponsored the event, and a Christian message would be presented. We felt good about that, even though the elders were not completely pleased. I remember the looks of the faces of the students that were moved by the presenter's message of hope, forgiveness, and acceptance available through a relationship with Jesus, that their attendance at the show was not by accident. They were brought there by God and needed to make that final move, that final choice to accept all that God had to offer by accepting Jesus as their Savior and Lord. It was a great night.

BEGINNING OF THE DEVIL

In many, if not all Christian theological frameworks, the Devil is a distinct individual. According to the Old Testament, after God created everything; the sun, stars, Earth, plant life, animals, and humankind, God decided to make one creature that was more beautiful, and more intelligent than all the rest. In a sense, he saved the best for last and put forth great effort to create this magnificent being and bestow on him incredible beauty and power. However, it appeared this being was not happy, even though he had everything at his disposal. He wanted more.

As the story goes, at some point, this individual wanted to be in charge of everything, even his Creator. He attempted a coup with other spiritual creatures in order to expel the reigning power and be the supreme force in the universe. Unfortunately for him, he underestimated the all-powerful God and was cast out of heaven along with all his cronies. This banishment took place in an instant like a lightning bolt hitting the ground. Jesus mentioned that he was there and saw it happen. His statement, while providing some insight on this event, also supported the divine nature of Jesus by placing him at the scene of Creation. From that moment on, this banished individual declared war on God and his angelic followers. The original name of this person/entity was derived from the planet Venus, which some translate to "the light of the morning" or "the shining one," literally translated as Lucifer. His spiritual army was comprised of the same spiritual beings as the angels but in their "fallen" state, now called demons.

Until my junior year in college, I had no direct contact with any demonic forces, nor did I know anyone who had. I was familiar with the red-horned pitch fork-toting bad guy that came out during Halloween and the angel on one shoulder and devil on the other scenarios. These images and stories were the only information I had, no direct experience on the topic.

The first significant impressions of evil I experienced was in college. The dorm I was in was the largest all-male dorm on campus. One weekend around Halloween, the Resident Assistances on each floor got the idea to run the movie *The Exorcist* a few times that Saturday night. The film was released a few years earlier. At church and during youth group meetings, we had all received stern warnings not to see it, as doing so would thereby support the Devil, in addition to exposing ourselves to possible harm. I did not know what that meant exactly, but it was enough for me to avoid the movie. That Saturday night, while the movie was showing, I sensed a heavy and dark presence in the dorm. Even then, I wondered if it was my preconceived ideas about the film I was projecting or an actual evil force — a tough call.

This brought up one of the other nagging questions I had wondered about for years. If God was all-powerful, then what did I, a believer, have to be concerned about? How could evil be bestowed on a Christian who had accepted Jesus as their Savior? This was farther reaching than the age-old question of how bad things could happen to good people. It also related to questions about if and how Christians could lose their Salvation, be harmed, or possessed by the Devil or a demon. I had learned that once you became a Christian, and Jesus enters your heart and mind, you are completely protected. It would be impossible for you to change your mind and commitment to God. I had also heard the opposing view that God would allow you to change your mind if you wanted to forfeit your eternal life. Some Christians from the Pentecostal perspective believe that a second experience was needed to "really" be a Christian and that was to accept the Holy Spirit. This experience was often confirmed by some miraculous sign like speaking in tongues or seeing visions. According to them, after you received the Holy Spirit, nothing could harm you. Still another perspective supported the idea that if you provided a "foothold" for the Devil, he could enter your heart and mind and bring it to destruction. The foothold could come in the form of alcohol or drug abuse, or exposure to pornography. In more extreme Christian circles, the list was longer and thus forbade things like dancing, listening to rock and roll music, smoking, and any form of physical contact with the opposite sex.

I was not convinced a person's behavior would provide an open door to the Devil, but I was wary of being around demonic images. Some could be scary, and after all, there was no conclusive evidence or consensus that a Christian could not be possessed. There is a story in the New Testament about some of Jesus's followers attempting to exorcise a demonic spirit from a man. They commanded the spirit in the name of Jesus and Paul to leave. The spirit spoke out saying that it knew Jesus and Paul, but didn't know who they were, so the possessed man physically beat up the followers until they left "bleeding and naked." Whatever the case regarding my protection or vulnerability, I was hesitant about even being around anything demonic.

What I didn't know was I would be exposed to demonic forces another way.

POSSESSION PART 1

I was dating a girl I had met through a friend at an IV summer retreat. Her name was Diane, and she lived about two hours away from my home in New Jersey. We spent a lot of time together that first summer. But the fall brought a move back to my upstate home-away-from-home in Rochester, another five hours away. That meant our relationship transitioned to the long-distance model, with much time spent on the phone and planning for the next time we would be together. Diane was a dark-haired, quiet girl, sweet and sincere. She was a born-again Christian, and we enjoyed talking about God, the Bible, and our faith. She attended Rutgers University at the Livingston campus in central New Jersey. While the school had an excellent academic reputation, campus life was known to be quite lively with many parties on the weekends hosted by fraternities, sororities, and in the dormitories. Alcohol and drugs were abundant, accompanied by loud music blasting at all the parties. One weekend close to Halloween, several large parties were planned, with posters mandating "costume required," and with "drinking to excess" assumed. For Diane and a few friends, that was when it happened.

I answered the phone a little after 1:00 AM on Sunday.

"I didn't wake you, did I?" she asked with some hesitancy in her voice.

"No, I had to get up to answer the phone," I replied.

"That's good. Something happened tonight, and I have to tell you about it." She spoke faster than usual.

My disappointment that she didn't laugh at my lame joke turned quickly to concern. What happened? I thought. Did she go to one of these parties? Did she hook up with someone? Did she accidentally drink some concoction?

"I was at a small group meeting with Katie and about six other people..." she started.

Ok, that's not too bad, I thought. No partying. It was a typical Intervarsity small group meeting. But maybe she met someone else. That's just great. She meets the love of her life, and I'm three hundred miles away, not scheduled to see her for months. This was "the" phone call. I just knew it. Interrupting my self-centered internal monologue, she continued.

"We met for our regular Saturday night small group meeting. This time in one of the meeting rooms in my dorm," she said.

"We were all sitting at the table with our Bibles and study guides, ready to begin the meeting. Right after I opened with a short prayer, I noticed Leslie, the girl across from me, was acting a little weird. She was looking around the room with a puzzled look on her face. Her eyes blinked and fluttered as if she had woken up and didn't know where she was. Then she began to move awkwardly in her chair, twitching slightly. I looked over at Katie to see if she noticed. Her eyes were wide with surprise. The person next to Leslie put her hand on her shoulder to see if she was alright just as Leslie began to move. But it didn't look like Leslie anymore."

"What do you mean?" I asked.

"It was Leslie, but she looked somehow different than Leslie. I can't explain it. A lot of it was her eyes." she explained,

"What do you mean her eyes?"

"It was like her eyes changed somehow, I mean they didn't physically change, but every time I looked at her eyes, I just got this powerful feeling of lightness and peace. They were beautiful, captivating, just beautiful . . ." She paused for a moment. "I'm sorry," she said, her voice breaking up with a soft whimper, "you must think I'm crazy, I'm sorry for this; it's so late."

"Diane, don't worry about it, you're not crazy." I tried to comfort her from hours away, at the end of a long phone cord, sitting in the hallway just outside my dorm room, to not wake my roommate. "The important point is that you're okay, right? Nothing bad happened?"

Diane continued as if she didn't hear what I just said., "And when she, or it, moved, it was more like she floated."

"Floated?" I asked skeptically.

"I mean she was walking, it wasn't like she was off the floor or anything, but she glided more than walked," Diane explained. "Beautiful, beautiful eyes," She repeated.

Diane continued to explain how Leslie seemingly glided around the room, just behind the others seated at the table. She said they all were confused and didn't know what was happening.

"Then, the thing began to speak." Diane continued. "The voice that came out of Leslie's mouth was definitely different than her normal voice. It had a soft tone, with a mix of feminine and masculine qualities. It came across as compassionate and reassuring. When it spoke, it referred to us as 'my children,' knew details of our lives."

"What details?" I asked, wondering if Leslie could have worked in Admissions part-time, and had access to student files.

"The names of family members, or how we were doing in school," she said, confirming some of my suspicions. "It also knew the Bible really well, quoting verses from both the Old and New Testament, citing chapter and verse," she added.

Then Diane told me that a few of the students began asking questions to understand better what this thing was. Many of its responses were vague.

"Where do you come from?" someone asked.

"From the beginning of time," was the soft response.

Then someone asked the question that most likely was on everyone's mind.

"How do we know if you are good or bad?" a girl from the group asked.

The response was strange.

After the student posed the question, it slowly approached Diane and gently lifted a silver cross she wore on her neck.

"Do you know who died on this cross?" asked the entity.

"Jesus Christ, the Son of God," Diane said, looking up at its captivating eyes.

"That's right," came the response, wrapped in velvety tones and a smile.

ANGEL IN TRAINING

Diane told me the session ended with many of the students feeling blessed to have such a close encounter with God. Some students said it felt like God was talking through Leslie; others thought it was an angel. A couple of her friends expressed skepticism and told Diane they were not sure if it was a good thing.

I stayed on the phone with Diane lasted for at least three hours. I couldn't believe how late it was. The other thing I couldn't believe was that during the entire conversation, tears were flowing from my eyes. I wasn't sad or upset, just listening and trying to understand what happened, but for some reason, my eyes gushed with tears.

I was perplexed by the story but didn't feel like Diane was in danger. Maybe it was because of the entity's gentle demeanor and that nothing dramatic occurred. No spinning heads or projectile vomiting. There was one strange thing that happened to Leslie that was disconcerting. Just after the meeting, she had an uncontrollable urge to run. Not just a jog but run as fast as she could around the campus for several minutes to the extent that she collapsed with extreme exhaustion. She didn't remember much of what happened. It was like a dream. Overall, Leslie felt at peace about it. She wasn't scared in any way. She knew that something happened and remembered parts of the conversations, but it was fragmented. She was surprised when the others told her what they witnessed and wondered why it happened to only her.

Another week flew by, and the next Saturday night I received another late-night call. It was from Diane again. They had had another meeting.

POSSESSION PART 2

The same group of students met again and, just as in the first meeting, shortly after they began, Leslie's eyes fluttered, and her body changed posture slightly. Diane told me that the captivating eyes were back. The same calmness and serenity returned too. The students continued to ask about events in their lives, similar to people asking a fortune teller or clairvoyant. The entity provided answers that included some specific details about events, but it also made statements that were hard to understand.

"Did you ask it about me?" I blurted at one point, unable to stop myself from asking.

"Yes, I did," Diane said warmly.

"Well, wha . . .what did you ask? What was the question? And what did it say?" I sputtered.

"I asked her, 'What about my boyfriend, Scott? Can you tell me anything about him?'"

The entity said, "I'll take care of the men in your life."

What the heck did that mean? I guessed it was good if the . . . thing . . . entity . . . spirit was good.

ANGEL IN TRAINING

Nevertheless, it sent shivers up and down my spine to think what it meant if it wasn't of God. And that was the debate occurring between more of the students. Was this a good thing or a bad thing? Was the entity from God, or an angel, or God himself? Or was it a demon or Satan himself?

Just like the week before, the call lasted nearly three hours. And, just like the last call, it caused me to tear uncontrollably as I listened to what happened. I didn't feel sad, I was listening to Diane explain what happened that night. The session was very similar to the one before with the entity talking with several of the students telling them about their lives.

My concerns were growing because the entity's answers were not profound; they were superficial and, according to Diane, at times, lacking any apparent meaning. The compulsion for Leslie to run after the experience was unsettling as well. Something was off, and although Diane seemed not to be adversely affected in any way, I did not like where this was going. I prayed that God would protect all the students, especially Diane, and somehow that the group would get to the truth of the matter.

During the next week, Diane was in contact with a few of the students who scheduled a meeting at a nearby church they had been attending in order to get another perspective. They told her they spoke to the pastor and a few of the elders, providing all the details of the two meetings. After considering all that had happened, the church leaders concluded the entity was not of God, and any further experiences should be avoided. They explained that they had made this determination based on three aspects of the event. The first was that nowhere in the

Bible had God or angels possessed a person. Secondly, it seemed the act of this possession could physically harm Leslie after the spirit left her body when she ran to exhaustion. Lastly, the content of what the entity was providing did not provide clear details compared to what the Christian tradition defined as "prophecy" of specific events but spoke in vague terms more commonly found in fortune-tellers and soothsayers.

Diane explained that when the students asked about the captivating appearance and soothing demeanor felt so powerfully by everyone in the room, the elders referred to the origin of Lucifer being a most beautiful creature, the Angel of Light. The elders also were not impressed by this spirit's knowledge of the Bible either. Any demon or evil spirit had more than adequate abilities to know every chapter and verse in the Bible and recite it accurately.

The other fascinating point was when one of the students brought up the response the entity had to whether it was good or bad. The elders explained that this answer further raised their suspicions of the nature of this creature by asking, "Do you know who died on this cross?" Of course, the Devil and all the evil forces agreed that Jesus died on the cross. That was their moment of triumph. The great truth was what happened three days later, when Jesus rose from the dead and conquered sin. This part was left out of the response. Obvious in its absence, according to the elders.

In the following days, disagreements in the group grew to the point where everyone agreed there would be no more meetings. Leslie was the only person who wanted the visitations to continue, even though the entity's origin was in question. Diane thought Leslie might have been attracted to the feeling of the experience, and maybe the attention. Everyone else wanted her to stop.

I did not hear anything further about Leslie or the events that took place over those few weeks, and I was glad nothing terrible happened. Diane was able to move on with no hard feelings about the group. I was relieved.

Through these events, I learned a valuable life lesson. Whatever we think we know about the spirit world or rules that we believe to exist, good, bad, and unexplainable events can, and will, happen. As stated so well in the famous play by Shakespeare:

> "There are more things in heaven and Earth, Horatio, than are dreamt of in your philosophy. Hamlet (1.5.167-8)

PUSH BACK

I graduated college a year after the possession incident and started working at a small graphic design studio in a busy part of northern New Jersey, about an hour from my parents. It felt good to be close to home, but far enough to be on my own. The long-distance took its toll on our relationship, and Diane and I stopped seeing each other. During my last year at RIT, I had wondered where I was going to end up. How would I know what job to take? I always prayed about it. Some of my prayers were, "Please God, show me the job I should take," or "Let me know which one is your choice for me." Unfortunately, there were no signs, voices, or visions of the future.

Some people say the reason why God does not let us see our future when we ask is that it would probably be upsetting. One reason is that we might see ourselves in an unfavorable situation. Another reason was because we would grow and mature over time and become involved in something far beyond our current capabilities. Seeing that future could cause tension or anxiety. My favorite prayer then and now, when presented with multiple options, is that the right choice will be obvious. Just as the choice for a

ANGEL IN TRAINING

college had been, with wrestling not being a primary interest and my doubts about attending a Christian college. That is precisely what happened when I found my first job after graduating from college. It seemed to be the only option.

I interviewed with several companies who offered me positions in different parts of the country. One position was with a large paper supplier in the mid-west. Another was with a commercial printing company in Chicago. The job I ended up taking was a sales position at a graphic design company. It was located in New Jersey and involved all my vocational interests in photography, commercial printing, and advertising. It was an obvious decision. However, being shy, insecure, and generally introverted, the choice of a sales position was a stretch for me. This stretch invoked much anxiety. I spent many nights praying for God to help me in upcoming meetings, getting new business, and overcoming objections from our customers. I retreated many times to the music and Bible verses that gave me comfort over the years at RIT. Bible verses that reminded me that God was all-powerful and heard my prayers. Sometimes, I would get an unexpected break at work, or I brought in a new client, or a current client called with a new project. In those times, I believed my petitions for God to help were answered. At the same time, I started to wonder, was it God answering my prayers or was it a result of my efforts? Who knew? I figured even if it wasn't divine intervention, my faith gave me the courage to do the things I needed to do to achieve results.

Even after a few weeks, I wasn't happy with my job. Although I was interested in graphic arts and photography, the job wasn't a passion for me. It was just a job. But I didn't want to live at home and needed the money.

As I began to settle into my new life, I visited a few nearby churches to try to meet fellow Christians. I got recommendations from friends of local churches that were Bible teaching and Evangelical. I tried a few but wasn't motivated to come back. I always felt like an outsider. I wanted to grow and learn just as I did at RIT, but I couldn't find any groups that felt right. I visited with old school buddies when they came to the area, but that was about it.

I heard about a correspondence school out of Chicago and thought that by studying the Bible in a more in-depth way, I would feel God's presence more in my life and not be as lonely. I took a few courses about Bible study methods and the New Testament theology. I enjoyed the studies immensely and began thinking about someday following in X's footsteps and becoming a minister.

Not too long after I began my job, some of my co-workers asked me to hang out with them after work. They were all young, and most of them were single. When I didn't join in their conversations about partying and college life, they asked me what I did for fun. As you might have guessed, telling them about going home after work to get started on a new Bible study correspondence course fell like a lead balloon. As usual, I got the strange looks and tentative reactions I had come to know from living in the dorms at RIT when someone from down the hall would burst into my room asking for a "f'ng pencil" and see three of us, heads bowed in prayer. The good thing is that I like people and have a good sense of humor. I generally build a good rapport with most people and had a lot of laughs with colleagues at my new job.

ANGEL IN TRAINING

Once, a few weeks before Christmas, several of us were finishing a meeting, and we were discussing what we were going to do for the upcoming holiday season. One discussion came around to religion, and a question surfaced. Does a person have to go to church to go to heaven? Knowing I was a religious person, all eyes turned to me, and my heart raced. Maybe this was an opportunity to witness to these people? It hadn't been on my mind as much, but as Christians, we were always supposed to make the best of every opportunity to spread the Gospel.

"Well, no. It's not the most important thing that you have to do . . ." I replied, trying to think of how best to word my next statement. I just went for it. "But you do have to know Jesus as your personal Savior in order to be saved." Inwardly, I winced as if I just threw a hand grenade into a crowd, waiting for the explosion.

"What?" blurted Paulann, one of my co-workers, cutting through the chatter. Paulann was a green-eyed, red-haired, direct woman in her late twenties who let no thought go unspoken. "That's it?" she said incredulously, "That's the only way to heaven? What about other religions? What about Jewish people?" she asked with exasperation in her voice, looking right at me with her penetrating eyes as she placed her computer back on the table.

Oh God, I thought, this is not going to be pretty.

I had my reply ready but was torn about using it with Paulann because she was the type of person that would not stand for ambiguity in any form from anyone. But, I let my standard answer fly. "The Bible says there is no other way except through Jesus. If you don't accept Jesus as your savior, you will go to hell. I know it sounds bad, but the good side is that the Bible says that 'anyone' can accept him. No one is excluded from this offer."

"But you're saying that you have to be a Christian to go to heaven, everyone else is going to hell." This time Paulann's voice raised a notch like she could not believe what she was hearing. During this exchange, a few people left the room, while a few others stayed and came to our side of the room to listen to the conversation.

"Well, yes, but it's open to everyone, all religions, and all people. God does not care where you came from, but all can come back to Him, through believing in Jesus."

"What do you mean 'Come back to him?'" she asked, sitting back in her chair. Her features softened, and her voice sounded a little less agitated. This was a good sign. She was not fighting it as much now. Maybe she would become a Christian after I explained everything, I thought.

"The Bible says we are all born in sin, separated from God, and we need a way to get back to Him. God provided a way by sending his son Jesus Christ to die on the cross to take away our sins and join with God now and in Heaven." I explained. More people walked out of the room, leaving only about four of us around the conference room table.

"Why were we all born in sin?" she asked.

"We just were. The Bible says it," I replied.

"What happens if we don't believe that whole sin part and believe that helping others as best you can and being the best person you can be is all you have to do?" she asked.

"That's not enough, according to the Bible. It says we are like sheep and have gone astray and the free gift of God is eternal life through Jesus. No one comes to God except through Jesus Christ," I continued. "Suppose you have a deadly disease and there is only one antidote. All you have to do is ask for it, and you will be saved."

"But what if I don't happen to want your antidote? What if I don't believe I'm sick?" she asked.

"Then whose fault is it? It's not the maker of the antidote. If a person dies who has had access to the antidote but rejected it, it's their own fault that they died, their own pride that caused them to reject the free gift that would save them. It's not God's fault when someone rejects Him, and they find themselves in Hell. They chose to be there because they were stubborn and selfish by not accepting his gift." I felt good. I had delivered the message beautifully, especially with that excellent antidote analogy. Maybe this was just the right time in her life to receive the Gospel

"So, it's 'my way or the highway' according to you. If someone does not believe what you believe, they go to hell, no matter what," she blurted, her demeanor tightening. Not a good sign.

"Well, if you think of it as 'there is only one way' it sounds terrible, but if you think of it as 'it's available to all,' it seems much better," I said, hoping to turn this around.

"But you are saying that everyone has to be a Christian to go to Heaven! You can start out in another religion, but in the end, you have to be a Christian," she said.

"It is what the Bible says; it says that we are sinners, and we need to get back to God. Jesus is the way back. He is the answer. It is not my idea. It's what the Bible says," I replied. I tried to look as positive as possible even though I knew this sounded harsh to Paulann.

She looked at me for a long moment. I wondered what she was thinking. There were still a couple of people in the room taking in this spirited exchange, but no one else said a word. I had no idea if she was accepting the Gospel as I presented it or not. Finally, in a calm voice, she spoke.

"You know Scott. You are such a nice guy. You're fun to be with, you talk with everyone about their lives, and you care about them. You have a lot of fun and make people laugh. But this . . . this take on religion and God . . . it's not you. It's too harsh and extreme. It can't really be part of who you are."

I was taken aback. At first thought, I could understand what she was saying. I'm sure it did seem very different from how I was in other aspects of my life. I wasn't so extreme about anything else and I generally respected differences in opinion for the most part. But it was the truth, and I knew it, and I had that confirming experience. There was no other way to God.

"The only thing I know is that I wanted to know the truth about God. I looked and looked and found the truth in Jesus," I said.

"I think you should keep on looking," she said abruptly, as she picked up her things and left the room.

Her statement stayed with me for many years. It was unsettling, a loose end, a festering issue, just under the surface.

IMPLOSION OF X

I was about two years into my first job out of college when I got the call. Something happened with X. Mom was upset. Dad was beyond angry. X sent them a letter that few parents receive and no parent anticipates. It was six pages long, beginning by saying he had been upset about some things in his life. X went on to explain that the main reason he was upset was Mom and Dad did not understand him. He explained that he knew he was different from most people. He was more sensitive, introspective, and thought deeply about almost everything. X wrote that he did not like when Mom and Dad tried to get him to be involved with us and interact with the rest of the family. And, when they gave him space to do what he wanted, he resented being ignored.

Not too long after we received the letter, X spoke with Mom and Dad on the phone and further explained how he was negatively impacted growing up in our family. He detailed several situations where Mom or Dad treated him poorly and resulted in lasting damage. Surprisingly, I was at one of the life-molding incidences he described.

I was in elementary school, and X was in high school. Mom and Dad were getting ready to go out to dinner with friends and X and I were in the living room playing with Lincoln Logs. We wanted to build a farm with a large barn and a fenced-in area for our cattle.

Mom was putting on her coat and said, "Okay, we're leaving. We'll be back by 9:00. And remember, I'm expecting an important phone call tonight. I left a pad and pencil by the phone to write down what they say. Okay?"

"Yes," X replied, half paying attention to what she said. He and I were figuring how to place the roof on a large structure.

Not too long after they left, the phone rang. X and I were still working on this now elaborate miniature community. X got up and came back. After some time, we finished our building project and then watched TV.

It was a little after 9:00 and after my bedtime. X and I were watching a TV show. As usual, I was playing possum, not moving or talking, which increased my chances that people would forget I was up past my bedtime. Mom and Dad came in through the kitchen door from the garage. Dad was humming his nondescript tunes as he always did, and Mom opened the hall closet to hang up their coats.

"Butch, did they call? I don't see a note," she asked casually.

X replied, just as casually "Yeah, they called, but I forgot what they said. I didn't write it down because we were . . ."

"You didn't write it down?" Mom yelled at a level I never heard before. Even the dogs outside began barking. "I told you it was an important call!" She screamed again, sounding like she was going to cry.

"You can call them tomorrow," X suggested. Big mistake.

"No, I can't call them, they aren't going to be around," she said as she stormed upstairs to her room.

Apparently for X, this was an unnecessary traumatic event because he simply forgot to write down a message. From his perspective, his own mother turned on him and unloaded her wrath on her sensitive son. She should have known that her reaction would be devastating for him. She should have known that it would scar him . . . scar him for life.

For the reasons outlined in the letter, X asked not to be contacted in any way. No phone calls, letters, drop by visits, nothing. What was missing in his letter was any responsibility on his part for his unhappiness, it was all us. This behavior is typical of a narcissistic personality, so self-involved they are unable to see past themselves. I saw how much his words and actions deeply hurt Mom and Dad. Mom had a hard time talking about it for several years, and Dad started to boil anytime the subject was raised. This impacted me quite a bit too because X was, to a large degree, my role model and my hero. Even more so, we were brothers twice. What the heck happened?

One possible explanation that led up to X's implosion could have been because his personal life and belief system came crashing down not too long before. His problems began after he graduated from King's College, the Christian school in New York. He then enrolled in another school steeped in conservative Christian thinking, Gordon-Conwell Theological Seminary located in Massachusetts. This school was not affiliated with any mainline denominations and recruited many of the faculty from conservative Evangelical schools such as Fuller Theological Seminary, Trinity Evangelical Divinity School, all of which centered on the same core beliefs. The core beliefs were that Jesus Christ was the only way of salvation and the Bible was the inspired Word of God, reliable, and without error. Their perspectives also required a literal interpretation of the entire Bible; meaning that all the stories about the creation, escapades of the prophets of the Old Testament, and accounts of the New Testament were authentic and had actually happened. As in many of the Evangelical circles, not only in education but in some of the churches as well, members had to sign a Statement of Faith indicating you espoused these tenets. Everyone had to sign this in order to be accepted.

Throughout his time at Gordon-Conwell, X learned about the lives and events in the Old Testament prophets. The perspective taken by the school was all these people were real, and the events actually occurred. As in any academic setting, theological and historical writings from this perspective were studied from numerous authors and scholarly texts collected over the centuries.

While the concept of Biblical reliability and literal interpretation can be at first viewed as a minor distinction, for some, it is a weighty topic. It speaks to the validity of religious beliefs, traditions, and the nature of God. If the texts explaining a faith's teachings are deemed unreliable, many people believed it placed their complete faith in question. Even more so, for people who must "know" conclusively, definitively, and without a doubt about God, this raises the stakes to an extreme level. If the Bible is questioned in any way, life as they know it could be forever changed. So, for those of us that needed constant reassurance that the Bible was the Truth, the Whole Truth, and nothing but the Truth, the Bible had to be true in its entirety and without error. If one started to think that the creation account was an allegory, or that David didn't really fight Goliath, for some, it could be the start down a road of their own destruction. After that, you might question the virgin birth and the resurrection, and where would that get you? Nowhere good, that's for sure.

This was the perspective that X was deeply immersed in for about three years in graduate school. He carefully examined ancient texts, comparing them with extra-biblical material, and analyzing countless lines of scripture. I remember X saying that he had to learn German because a prominent theologian wrote a commentary on an Old Testament text and he had to read it first-hand, not by translation. This is the type of guy X is, extraordinarily detailed, and passionate about getting to the truth of things. He loved his time studying at Gordon Conwell and did exceptionally well academically. He excelled so far and loved it so much; he decided to continue to study at one of the nation's leading academic institutions for Near East Ancient History at the University of Chicago. Where else would someone like X go but to the school that produced the highest number of Noble prize winners in US history?

Unfortunately for X, his intensity and drive to understand the truth about God, his attachment and background in conservative Evangelical thinking, and his education at Chicago proved to be too much for him. His time in Chicago was the beginning of the end of our relationship with X.

What happened in Chicago took X entirely by surprise. As he began taking courses at the university, he discovered that he was operating with some assumptions about the Bible that were incompatible with what was taught at the Chicago school. The faculty of this prestigious institution did not believe some of the most basic concepts he had spent the last several years studying. The most significant assumption of X's that was challenged was the idea that the Bible was to be taken as literal truth. One example was related to Moses.

According to the Old Testament books, Moses was the person who rallied the Jews when they were being held captive by the Egyptians as slaves. He used the seven plagues to force the Pharaoh to give the Jews their freedom and escape into the desert. Moses was also the one who parted the Red Sea and later brought the Ten Commandments to them on the famous stone tablets. To X, Moses and everything he did was to be taken as historical fact and actual events. However, in the opinion of many of the scholars at the University of Chicago, the stories about Moses were contrived and, not only that, there was a good possibility a person named Moses never actually existed. Many of these scholars had multiple advanced degrees and had been teaching, conducting research, and publishing for many years. This perspective, held by both faculty and students, was something X could not handle. X said that a few fellow students laughed at him for believing what he did.

ANGEL IN TRAINING

X's reaction was extreme. Here he was at the pinnacle of his academic career with years of preparation to further his education, only to find that his academic superiors flatly denied some of his most basic assumptions. What happened? How had he gotten so far off course? Why had no one told him this? Apparently, the last question was the one he was most fixated on, the first wave of blame that began to boil. How could Gordon-Conwell not have prepared him for this? Why didn't they say that these perspectives were not only out there, but held by the some of the most prestigious institutions in America? How could they have let him down? The second wave of blame is what hit home for us, and mainly Mom and Dad. In the aftermath of X's discovery, he began to distance himself from the family. At first, it was unreturned phone calls or letters, which had Mom and Dad concerned. They tried to reach out to him with no response. Then it came, the letter asking not to be contacted. In the letter, he described why he came to this conclusion, as he believed it was his upbringing that did him in. He stated that living on our dead-end street and provincial town prevented him from not being open to other ideas.

Maybe he got a hold of some pop psychology book that proclaimed the bulk of our nature comes from our relationship with our mother. I don't know. What I do know is that it devastated Mom and Dad to read these words from their oldest son. The son with so much talent and drive to excel at everything, only to end up blaming them for all the things he felt he could not be.

My reaction was anger. How dare he! How could anyone blame their parents for their attitudes or traits? I could see if a child was abused or traumatized in some way, but not us; we weren't abused or raised in harsh conditions. He was the one who should have known that there might be people out there that didn't agree with Evangelical perspectives. What the hell? And, then to blame it all on Mom and Dad, mainly Mom? It was screwed up. He was screwed up. I kept thinking of Mom and how upset she was. Dad, too, although he did not say much. I wondered if X had been brainwashed at the seminary he attended. Because if he stayed there to become a minister, he never would have known other points of view existed. Then he would have been a minister, teaching others this same narrow view of God. In one way, it was good that he learned about other perspectives and maybe even that he blew up like that. At least he didn't go out in the world and teach other people his viewpoint and mess up their lives too.

    It took a long while for me to get over X's rejection of us, and as I did, my Christian beliefs changed significantly.

ONE STEP TO THE LEFT

Getting to know people outside of the conservative Christian circles at RIT, coupled with X's crisis and rejection of us, caused me to reconsider the all-or-nothing approach to religion. I thought about what my Gospel message did to my high school friendships. For the first time, I began to see a dichotomy emerging in my faith. The positive and accepting message wasn't always evident to others.

The exclusivist perspective was troubling, the idea of an all-loving God being angry if you didn't come to him in a specific way. The compassion of Jesus, and the strength and comfort of a Father-God figure that had helped me in so many lonely, needy, and hopeless times contrasted with the idea of a jealous or vindictive God. X's reaction was the last straw for me. I didn't know anyone smarter or more passionate about religion, theology, or God. To see him collide with people who were just as smart as him, only to crumble, blame his parents, and eject himself from our family, called everything I thought we believed into question. The Truth should be stronger than this. I could see now that something wasn't right about the Christian message, at least as I understood it. I wrestled with it because it did still make a lot of sense to me. The Christian message accounted for everything: the beginning of sin, the nature of man, the salvation message, and the removal of sin. It was all there, complete and straightforward. Maybe it was my beliefs that had to be tempered. But how? How could I do that without betraying the gospel?

After a few years of not attending any church regularly, I found a nearby Presbyterian church. In my undergrad days, the Presbyterian faith had been way too liberal for us to tolerate. Depending on the area of the country, the Presbyterian faith made some departures from the inerrancy question in addition to allowing women more leadership responsibilities. They even permitted homosexuals to join the church, which was generally unacceptable in conservative Christian groups. Initially, these reasons raised a red flag for me, and I suspected they were not holding strictly to the Christian faith.

However, this church was different from any other church I had attended in many ways. The moment you walked in, you felt welcomed. The pastor was a genuine and lively person. I attended the church for several weeks and started to think that this best mirrored where I was in my faith's journey. They were certainly Christian and Bible-based, but not to the extreme I had been accustomed. They taught that the Bible was true and that the only way to heaven was through a belief in Jesus, but it wasn't the first or only message presented. The graciousness, love, and compassion of God were the most important messages in the sermons.

The building itself followed in the traditional architecture of ornate cathedrals containing polished wood pews and tremendous wooden beams anchored overhead. The walls were paneled with dark wood as well as with stained glass windows down the side of the church and over the entrance. The sanctuary contained an enormous pipe organ with the pipes and decorative wooden framework filling the entire front of the room, looming behind the twin lecterns. The services were conducted formally with the leaders wearing robes and following a planned and detailed format. The outstanding difference to me was that this church presented a high level of formality and ritual as in my Lutheran upbringing but in an atmosphere of genuine care and love to all who walked through the doors. It was, and most likely still is, a warm and Godly place to attend. I quickly became involved in church activities and helped run the youth group, becoming good friends with the pastor and his family.

The Presbyterian tradition is academic. By that I mean there is little about the theology that has not been thought through carefully and steeped in historical and academic rigor. Presbyterianism differs from the original reformers like Martin Luther by adopting the more Calvinistic approach. The best analogy I learned was that Martin Luther took the current Catholic tradition and re-organized aspects to reflect God's original intentions, similar to rearranging clothes in a dresser drawer. Whereas John Calvin did far more than rearrange the clothes, he emptied all the drawers and started from scratch by reconstructing a tradition that best reflected God's nature and wishes for humankind. For example, one aspect of the Presbyterian Church structure is the idea that everyone will be given the opportunity to be heard, even at the highest levels of church organization. The method of doing this can be identified as the Roberts Rules of Order used by the government and many structured organizations around the world. The monitoring of power and influence was also brilliantly balanced. For example, two groups run each church congregation, the board of Deacons and the Board of Elders. The Deacons oversaw running the logistical operations of the Church, such as the grounds, building, and financial matters. The Elders were the spiritual leaders charged with overseeing the teaching, leadership, and direction of the church. The Elders were elected positions and rotated on the board, called the Session, in three-year terms. The Elders conducted the searches for the pastor and other leadership positions as needed. It is interesting to note that the pastor was not a voting member of the session, so is excluded from voting on all decision making. This places the power solely in the hands of the Elders while limiting the pastor to an influential role.

Initially, this was a settling-down time for me spiritually and emotionally. The church professed a strong allegiance to Christian beliefs but did not force or proselytize others to believe. It was up to God and the individual to work out the Gospel and Salvation on a timeline known only to God Himself. The pastor and I had a few discussions about the consequences of the hardline approach to religion. He told me he had counseled several people over the years that had a similar reaction as I had with the conservative interpretation of the Gospel and resulting emotional damage. I was greatly relieved to hear that because of my experiences with my friends and what I had observed with X.

In effect, I created a gray zone of possibility where the truth was. I blurred the lines. If someone asked me if a person went to hell when they died if they had not accepted Jesus, my answer was that God was fair. Perhaps right after death, He would reveal the salvation message, and if the person then rejected the Gospel, they'd be sent to hell. In either case, it was their decision to be saved or enter into eternal punishment. That position felt right to me, it didn't conflict with what I believed about the way of Salvation and it didn't present the hardline message either. I was in a good place.

SLOW BURN

Soon after I began attending the Presbyterian church, I began to teach the junior high school Sunday school classes, and was eventually elected and ordained as an Elder. I wanted to be a good Christian in every way possible because this was it, the way to live and navigate life most effectively. I went to church every Sunday and sometimes prayer services on Wednesday nights. I studied the Bible when I wasn't teaching Sunday school and attended adult classes.

I enjoyed teaching Sunday school and continued for about eight years. I used some Presbyterian guidebooks with fun exercises and activities to make learning about God and the Bible enjoyable. I especially enjoyed teaching about the origins of a variety of concepts such as sin, angels, the devil, the Bible, and salvation, among others. I took a conservative viewpoint, considering the Bible as truth. Except for this time, I left some of the controversial topics up to God, such as what happens to people who believe in other religions, if God loves homosexuals, and if the Bible is without error.

Life was good. I had finally found my niche in life. Everything made sense. I was doing the right things, and God was with me. I married a woman I met at my first job out of college and she and I started a graphic design business, as well as starting our family. First with a little boy, and then another, and then another. As with any household with young children, the house was filled with lots of energy, laughs, tears, and Band-Aids.

During this time, I made a second attempt to learn about God and the Bible by taking a few night courses at a nearby seminary, still feeling that someday I might go into the ministry. But something wasn't sitting right with me. Even though I was heavily involved with the church and raising a family, there was something amiss. And it was getting worse.

DECOMPENSATION

Part of what was bothering me at church was pure burnout. I was in my mid-thirties, serving as an elder, teaching Sunday School, and helping at many of the special events. At one point, I noticed the 80/20 rule was in play. Twenty percent of us were doing eighty percent of the work. I was tired.

As far as I knew, God was in our lives. When the stress of running the business started to get to me, I prayed and prayed for help. One time we needed a few thousand dollars for a down payment on a printing production job for a new client due that Monday. We didn't have it and none of our present clients were due to send a payment. All weekend I prayed, asking God to provide some way out of this. I was surprised and relieved when Monday's mail brought a check for well over what we needed. A client paid a bill early.

Even with a few of these remarkable events occurring now and then, a level of unhappiness was creeping into my life. It began as an unsettling feeling. I felt empty. I tried to ignore my feelings by focusing on all the things I was doing for the church and my spiritual growth, attending prayer meetings, attempting to take Bible study classes, fasting from time to time, memorizing hymns, and other religious rituals.

Communion at the church was always a special time for me, and I welcomed those Sundays when it was offered. The pastor at this church conducted an exceptional service that combined the reciting of scripture, well-known gospel hymns, and time to reflect on God's love and power that enveloped us all in the room. This was truly a moving experience with the pipe organ playing softly in the background and the bounding, deep and reassuring voice of the pastor proclaiming:

> "Jesus said 'let all men come unto me, and I will give them rest,'" pausing after each statement.
>
> "Jesus said, 'cast your burden on me for my burden is light'"
>
> "Jesus said, 'come unto me all who are heavy laden, and I will give you rest'"
>
> "Jesus said, 'for God so loved the world that he gave his one and only Son, that whoever believes in him shall not perish but have eternal life.'"
>
> "Jesus said, 'Man shall not live by bread alone, but by every word that proceeds from the mouth of God'"

Many times, during these services, I was moved to tears and felt everything was going to be okay. Feelings of peace and contentment washed over me. God was in charge, and everything would be alright. But then Monday morning came around again, and the "small business owners' paradox" returned. This was when the stress of slow times and not having enough work was replaced with the stress of being too busy to meet deadlines. The pressure, in addition to general fatigue, fluctuation of cash flow, and caring for a young family, combined in a blanket of insecurity that became an unsustainable crushing weight. I was able to get a job at a large pharmaceutical company, which helped the cash flow, but the other stress factors were still in play.

Over this same period, unhappiness was creeping into my marriage as well. I didn't know precisely why it was happening, and it seemed like there was nothing I could do to stop it. My ongoing prayers yielded no results and the slow deterioration ended in divorce.

Around the time this was happening, I met with a counselor to learn how to cope with the situation and to help me figure out why this happened. After spending time hearing about what happened from my perspective, he startled me with his assessment.

"You are not going to like what I'm going to say, but in a way, you had a perfect marriage." He said confidently.

"I had a what?" beyond angry; I shot back. "That's what you got from what I told you about what went on over the last eight years?" I was about to walk out of the session.

"It's not the perfect marriage that you think," he said, "it's that you two were perfect for each other based on the families you came from and how they primed you to get together."

"I have no idea what you are talking about," I said, still agitated.

"I don't want to oversimplify what happened but let me sketch it out for you. Your ex-wife was raised in a male-dominated household. You, on the other hand, were the youngest child in a home of strong-willed individuals. Your mom and your siblings all told you what to do and when to do it. Everything was fine as long as you did what everyone told you to do. You resented always being the tag-a-long, the one with least important things going on in your life.

Then it happened. You two met, and it was magic. She finally met a male that would listen and do whatever she wanted, and you were very comfortable slipping into the subservient role you had lived with your entire life. The problems started when you began asserting your individuality. Neither of you knew what was going on, both of you were unknowingly battling the demons of your past. Unfortunately, the demons won."

ROCK BOTTOM

My divorce unraveled me on a profound level. I viewed the family as the pinnacle statement of one's life, and now I was merely visiting the house I had worked so hard to make our home. One of the most painful parts of the divorce was walking into "my" house and feeling like an outsider. Knocking at the front door and entering like I was a guest, and then looking around at the rooms I renovated and the walls I painted. I heard once about something called "the picket fence syndrome" where a person grieves the loss of the home scenario; the house, home, and family life. I found myself feeling that regularly. Our front porch had a white picket fence with a gate that needed periodic adjusting to work well. Sometimes, when I was waiting for the kids to answer the door when I came to pick them up, I fixed the gate.

More importantly, my family breakup struck at the root of what I believed about God. How could this have happened? Specifically, how could it have happened to me? How did I get it wrong? I could see how it could

ANGEL IN TRAINING

happen to a guy who worked all the time, went out drinking and carousing with his friends, coming home drunk, or lost his job because he didn't show up for work. But I was an Elder, for God's sake, a Sunday school teacher, involved with the church, deeply committed to seeking God on a personal level, longing to know him better. On top of that, I had several avenues of connection to God through friends at church, many times of worship, and my spiritual rituals. It didn't make sense to me. I had no idea why or how it happened. I was devastated, lost, angry. . . defeated.

It's not that I was angry at God, although there was an element of that at times. I was more upset at myself and began to question my beliefs about God and if my expectations about how he was "supposed" to help us were valid. Maybe there wasn't a God. Maybe it was just a nice idea that people made up to cope with life. Maybe it didn't matter what you did with your life because there was nothing out there, no one that cared or intervened when asked. I visited a few nearby churches but did not make any connections, and the Presbyterian church was too far away.

My anger smoldered and turned into a depression that began to overtake me. I was living alone in a town 45 minutes from my children and 10 minutes from my job. I managed to get out of bed, get dressed, and to work each day. At least work got my mind off things for a few hours and provided some stability in my life. But still, the strain of the loss of the picket fence, questions about all the time and effort I spent pursuing God over the years, and financial devastation began wearing on me.

During the second year after I moved out, I entered a dark time. I began drinking regularly and heavily, mostly wine and especially on the weekends when I didn't have the kids. Many times, I even drank during the week. It helped mask the pain and let me forget about things, at least enough to get through the nights. People offered platitudes such as to "not lose heart," or "this too shall pass," "the first two years are the hardest," and "there's a light at the end of the tunnel." Blah, blah, blah. I appreciated their sentiments, but they were of no help. When you are in that kind of pain, no words from anyone can help.

One night I hit rock bottom. It was two days away from a court date to settle financial aspects of the divorce, and my attorney, as usual, was not returning my calls. I felt exceedingly powerless and depressed. It was raining, and the last straw was my HBO had been turned off. I had been receiving it for free since I moved in because it was never turned it off when the previous tenant left. A new tenant had moved in below me, and I guess the cable company audited the building and discovered that I was receiving it erroneously. Although it may seem trite, it was a big deal to me, especially on top of everything else. At least I had my HBO to watch. The kids were young, not teenagers yet, and got excited too. Now and then I overheard them talking to a friend saying, "We have HBO at Daddy's."

Feeing the way I did, I resorted to my staple feel-good solution. I walked around the corner to the liquor store and purchased two bottles of my favorite Australian red wine, Rosemont Shiraz, and returned to my apartment. Not too far into the second bottle, I was feeling the welcome numbness that had become familiar over the last year.

Only this time, I sank deeper into a sea of depression and hopelessness. Where could I turn now? There was nothing. My friends gave me well-intentioned platitudes and God . . . well, God was MIA if he'd ever been there at all. I had nothing.

The rain let up around midnight, and I was almost done with the second bottle. It was a warm night, and I contemplated another run to the wine store for one more bottle, but the liquor store was closed. Damn! Well, that was it; I remember thinking. I exhausted all my resources for feeling good, and there was nothing on the horizon that was bright. I had to work the next day but why should I bother, considering I gave most of my money to my ex anyway? There was one other thing.

I had a life insurance policy that would put my kids in good stead for the future. What a great parting act, I thought. I could end the pain and provide for my kids all at once. I had a motorcycle I'd purchased a few years earlier. My ex-wife and her family hated it, but I was a biker through and through and rode when I could. It was a red and white Honda CB1100F, a beautiful and powerful street bike that could exceed 125 mph with no problem, as I knew from experience.

I lived near a major highway with lots of straightaways to get to maximum speed quickly. I had spent many hours on the Garden State Parkway over the years and thought now of the many bridges that crossed over the parkway, with their corresponding concrete pillars and walls. If I hit one of those going over 100 mph, I was confident I wouldn't make it. I had to pick the spot carefully because some of the concrete structures had grassy areas in front, and that could slow me down. There was one spot, not too far away, that was perfect.

This was the solution — finally, a plan, a way out for me and a future for my kids. The kids would have to deal with my loss, but they already had a rich guy in the home with their Mom's boyfriend. He was a nice guy, and they would have a bunch of money. I thought about the helmet. It might spare me. I could throw it off right before I hit. But, was there a suicide clause in the life insurance policy? If they saw the helmet was released yards before the crash site, blood alcohol level off the charts, and learn of my recent divorce, they would put two and two together and deny the claim.

It was a chance I would have to take. I would put my helmet on but leave it unstrapped, so it would easily fall off. Of course, the risk in all of this was the non-fatal injuries that could leave me severely disabled, requiring others to take care of me. Here I was wanting to end it all with no strings attached, providing one last gesture of life insurance money to my kids, and instead could end up being a burden for decades, not to mention enduring unending pain and operation after operation. Damn it. I didn't know what to do. But life is filled with tough choices. What hell, I thought. I'll do it.

I was sitting on the floor resting against the couch in front of the TV when I decided to put my plan into action. I could walk the mile to my friend's house where I kept my bike and go for one last ride. I stood, abruptly banging into the door jamb. Taking a few steps back, I ran into a different door jamb. The next thing I knew, the TV flashed past my eyes, and I felt a hard whack as the carpet hit my face. Okay, let's try this again, I thought, but slowly this time. I got to all fours, and slowly stood, steadying myself against the wall unit. I had the idea that I should call my friend and tell them I was coming over to get the bike. I picked up the wall phone and stared at the buttons. They were all blurry. Confirming that my glasses were on, I realized I was operating on two bottles of wine with a small lunch and no dinner.

"At least, whatever happens, it's not going to hurt." I thought. I glanced at the oven clock. 2:05 AM. I was glad I hadn't called. I decided to walk to the bike. When I headed to the door to leave, I found it locked. Try as I might, the door would not budge. Then I thought, "But I'm on the inside; this shouldn't be happening." Ahh, the deadbolt was in. I reached for my keys to unlock it, only to remember that no keys were needed, just a knob that needed turning to the left. As I pulled the door, it seemed to burst open with a force, just missing a direct hit to my head. When I stepped back out of the way, I tripped on the kitchen chair and felt the sharp thud of the cool linoleum floor hit the back of my head.

When I awoke, the morning light was streaming in the open front door, my head a few inches from the refrigerator, and all the lights and the TV on. A massive headache and stomachache were my first sensations. After vomiting for a while, I took a handful of Advil, a shower, and went to work.

That night was the starting point in reconstructing my life from the ground up. That had been ground zero. Something, and to this day, I'm not sure what it was, but something deep inside me formed a firm ground to stand on emotionally. Even with no real answers to what the future held, I knew nothing could be worse than what I just lived through. If I had been able to get to my bike that night, I most likely would have completed my plan. But I didn't, and I had a sense of relief that although I had gone to the precipice and looked deeply into the abyss, I had found something of myself. I felt as if I was now standing in the rubble of the burned-out building of my life.

It was also the first time I was standing on my own.

PART TWO
MOVING BEYOND RELIGION

LOOKING INTO THE ABYSS

I couldn't stop thinking about it. If I had been able to get to my bike that night, I might have completed my plan. To say the experience moved me deeply would be an understatement. It reminded me of the Nietzsche quote as portrayed in the movie *Wall Street* when the young, cocky, stockbroker, Bud Fox (Charlie Sheen), was arrested in his office on charges of insider trading. As the officials walked him out, his manager says to him, "When a man looks in the abyss, and nothing is staring back at him, at that moment, the man finds his character."

With no real answers about the future, the one thing I did know was that nothing could be worse than what I just experienced or what could have happened.

I slowly began to reconstruct what led me there. How did I get to that place? How could I reconcile the disconnect between my feelings and my faith? I had stopped going to church. I was torn between the positive feelings of the services, hymns, and prayers and the feelings of loss, betrayal, and confusion about what my "exemplary"

Christian life had produced. The guidance I received from my beloved religion had turned out to be bogus. My nagging doubts blossomed to full bloom. Nevertheless, in spite of all that had happened, I still had the drive to understand the nature of God and had an undeniable certainty there was something I was meant to learn.

Working through all that had happened; one of the first insights I arrived at was that there was a distinct possibility that it wasn't that God that let me down. The center of my problem was my perceptions of God.

I thought about this for a long time.

Where did I learn about God? From church for one, and from the many pastors, elders, and teachers I encountered over the years. I also learned about God from the Bible, specifically the Judeo-Christian version, and the many hours studying the Christian faith at churches and Christian organizations. I wanted to know more about how people developed perceptions about God, and to that end, I began exploring the psychology of religion and spirituality.

I was introduced to psychology at the seminary I attended when taking two courses in Pastoral Counseling. I was surprised to learn how often pastors got involved in personal counseling. The instructor told us the first person most people go to when they are experiencing emotional difficulties is their pastor, priest, rabbi, or other religious leaders. Through the coursework, I became familiar with some general psychological concepts—related to the nature of human emotion, human development, and learning theories. One common problem, from the perspective of the conservative Christian instructor, was that psychology approached life from a secular perspective. At that time, the idea resonated with me because we had been told many times how dangerous it was to venture away from the Bible. But I was in a different place now, and still drawn to the subject. Throwing caution to the wind, I signed up for a few general psychology classes at a nearby university.

Focusing my energy on subjects other than theology and religion was refreshing, and I quickly felt I was on solid ground once again. I was excited to learn about how the human mind worked, exploring various theories of nature, nurture, human development, and psychological disorders. I was surprised to learn that a few of the early psychologists started out studying religion or were raised in religious families and eventually abandoned their roots to study psychology. After a few years of taking evening classes, I earned my master's degree. Although many of my questions were still unanswered about God, me, and how to navigate through this life.

Throughout my coursework, I only saw a few instances where religion intersected with psychology and wondered why. One reason I learned was that psychology and religion got off to a bad start. The founders of modern psychology unequivocally portrayed any concepts of God as nothing less than delusional. Sigmund Freud, James Skinner, and Albert Ellis stated that religion contained "wishful illusions," "universal obsessional neurosis," and even claimed that people are healthier without religion.[1] Atheists and other opponents of religion used these statements to discount beliefs about God and religion. Prominent psychologists like Carl Jung, William James, and others disagreed, and presented positive views of religion and psychology.

I turned forty just after completing a master's degree,

and this milestone event helped to motivate me to continue my journey. I enrolled in a doctoral program in the school of psychology at Fielding Graduate University in California. I chose this school because of its excellent reputation, and it was the only distance learning school endorsed by the American Psychological Association. Unsure how this school approached the area of religion and spirituality, I was hesitant to declare my specific interests in spiritual development. To my surprise, I quickly learned the faculty wholeheartedly accepted my subject of inquiry. However, they cautioned me that a scientific investigation of spirituality could be a slippery slope because scholars interject their own biases, thus producing flawed research.

Nevertheless, I was more than ready to delve deeper into this murky academic realm. The university's course structure, together with the incredibly encouraging faculty, further motivated me to explore the topic of spirituality. The curriculum included mandatory core subject matter competencies but also allowed students to examine specific areas of interest, as long as it was within the scope of the class. This is how I was able to investigate many areas of interest to me, along with the required curriculum.

A significant realization came to me when I was trying to figure out what I wanted to learn. It wasn't just religion or theology. I had tried that in seminary and felt confined. The focus of my interest was on how people relate to and experience God. Realizing the beliefs I held about God caused many of my problems, I took the first step on my new journey.

Lesson 1 — We create our perceptions about God

COMMONLY CONFUSED TOPICS

The first topic I wanted to learn more about was the difference between religion and spirituality. I knew they were related, but the meanings were blurred. There are multiple definitions for both. In one instance, the focus of spirituality is defined as the connection to God, and religion was the way to provide that connection. Technically, the word religion means a belief, interest, or activities related to God. A natural tendency is to link the two, associating one specific religion with an ultimate, universal God. Another description of the two terms is that religion relates to outward, observable behaviors and actions, and spirituality is internal and subjective. Along with that idea, Sandra Schneiders, Professor emerita in the Jesuit School of Theology at the Graduate Theological Union, defines spirituality as the integration of one's self "toward the ultimate value one perceives."[1]

Although spirituality and religion are straightforward concepts, blurring the differences between them can have profound implications.

Outward religious behaviors are activities such as church attendance, rituals, frequency of prayer, meditation, or any other action an individual associates with their beliefs. These behaviors are easy to observe and measure. For example, how frequently someone goes to church, synagogue, or mosque, or how many times someone prays, meditates, chants, and for how long. These are all outward behaviors. However, as we all know, they can be independent of what the person truly believes, thinks, or feels. We have all met or heard about religious people who participate in religious activities or are even revered as godly religious leaders but are later found to be unkind, abusive, or even criminal. These people might appear to be religious but would not score high on anyone's idea of being spiritual.

Levels of spirituality are harder to assess because they are associated with subjective internal states. There are a few validated surveys that attempt to measure characteristics of spirituality, such as the purpose and meaning of life, spiritual awareness, and integration of personality. Also, reliable measures have been developed to access an individual's level of spiritual integration. For example, frequency and content of prayer, in addition to an assessment of meaning in life, have been developed to detect changes in people as a result of acute spiritual experiences or spiritual development.[2,3] Understanding the different meanings between these terms is critical in becoming aware of our spiritual journey.

Learning this distinction helped me understand why some people are so intense about their religious beliefs. The beliefs contained in my conservative Christian religion explained God logically and pragmatically. The core system of Christianity and the Plan of Salvation provided an explanation of the Universe, my place in it, and why. My Evangelical Christian religion and my understanding of God were one in the same, and most importantly, I assumed universal.

THE PLAN OF SALVATION

- God made us perfect, but we (Adam) left him in the Garden of Eden.
- God wants to reconcile because of Adam's disobedience but can't because of God's perfect nature.
- Now we are born in sin, separated from him because of Adam's defiance.
- God has provided a way back to him through Jesus.
- Anyone who does not believe that Jesus is the only way will be sent to hell and tortured forever.

At one time, I thought anything challenging this construct was at the best suspect, and at worst, a threat to the fabric of heaven and Earth. As far as outward religious practices, different faiths varied to large degrees about what a person had to do to maintain a good relationship with God. My experience with this in the Christian fellowship group and Christian churches was that church attendance was crucial. Many times, church leadership used passive-aggressive comments to reminded everyone to come to church. "We haven't seen you for some time. Is everything okay?" Or in some congregations, calls would be made with specific directives to attend church or risk losing membership status. Certainly, the Catholic confession and penance ritual is an excellent example of how religious behavior is linked to your standing before God, according to the church. Other examples would be the Christian communion service or Muslim times of prayer.

The distinction between a person being religious and being spiritual becomes evident when we learn about religious people committing atrocities. The Crusades, the 100-year war, child abuse cases, sex scandals, mass murder, and suicides have been committed by religious and assumed spiritual people. This shows that it is possible to be a religious person and yet have no spiritual or Godly connection. This is not to say that religion has no meaning. Quite the opposite, as many times our spirituality can only be expressed through religious behavior.

An essential factor in the integration of the two concepts is that religious behaviors are emotionally linked to one's religious belief system. My beliefs brought me to God and God to me. I experienced times of peace and contentment going to Jesus in times of trouble. Also, the wonderful times participating in communion services brought me great comfort by helping me to remember I was on good terms with God. Other non-Christian ideas about God challenged those feelings and attacked my insecurities. That's why I thought the non-Christian beliefs had to be wrong.

When I initially accepted the conservative Christian beliefs, I could not fathom how anyone could not feel the same way I did about their religious beliefs. Especially when other belief systems did not teach that you needed a personal relationship with Jesus. Also, other religions did not explain so plainly how we could reconcile our sins. I reinforced this thinking many times over the years, spending countless hours learning about Christian theology and how other religions "erred" in their theology. One error was denying that Christ was God. This was a crucial point because if Christ was not God, then his death on the cross meant nothing and there was no viable plan of salvation. Other errors were allowing homosexuals to be leaders or relying on different texts and authors other than the Bible. At that time in my life, I thought that Christianity was still the most logical, rational, and truest of all religions.

From my perspective, the death of Jesus on the cross logically paved the way to our connection to God, and all the things we did to recognize and celebrate that fact confirmed it was real. It was *The Truth* for me. All other belief systems paled in comparison. It didn't take me long to realize my feelings of certainty stemmed from an emotional connection to my beliefs. Also, what increased my emotional stake was the mystical experiences I had encountered along the way. The born-again experience, the peace and contentment I sometimes felt when praying, and the calming and reassuring communion services.

These interactions of deeply personal emotions, tied to an organized belief system, is often the foundation of intense religious fervor. It fuels the disagreements, conflicts, and wars existing since the beginning of humankind. I could finally see exactly how this could be because I vividly remember thinking any other approach to God could not offer what I felt in my heart and knew in my mind. This was my foundation and my rock. Everything else was wrong, wrong, wrong.

At least until I met someone that got me thinking.

Lesson 2 — Religion and spirituality are two distinct concepts. A person can be religious without being spiritual and spiritual without being religious.

WHAT, WAIT ... THERE ARE OTHERS?

During the time I was working through these ideas, I met a woman around my age at work. She was a freelance writer we hired to assist on a few projects. I don't remember how it came up, but during a break, she mentioned she was a Buddhist. My defenses immediately went up. From what I had learned, Buddhists could not be more wrong when it came to understanding God. During my years in the Intervarsity Christian Fellowship at RIT, we learned how to poke holes in this belief system instantly. They didn't believe in an all-powerful deity, heaven, or hell. They believed in Jesus, but only as a popular teacher. They also believed in reincarnation, which was not supported in the Bible. The worst offense was that they did not see a need to be saved. According to Buddhism, each lifetime was a step toward enlightenment and lessons to be learned. One day you would "get it," become enlightened, and understand that everything, including you, were a part of God.

Typically, I would subtly lead the conversation to discuss the differences in our belief systems and explain why Christianity addressed the issues in the human condition more logically and completely than any other religion, especially Buddhism. For some reason, this time, I did more listening than talking. This might have been because this woman conveyed her thoughts with such sincerity and conviction; it encouraged me to listen. She told me how she was raised as a Buddhist but was also taught about other religions, including Christianity. She described the alter she had in her home, where she went to read and meditate. She told me how she relied on her Buddhist scriptures throughout her life because they conveyed stories of how other believers overcame suffering and pain.

As I listened, I was fascinated by how similarly we had experienced our religions. At one point, she had tears in her eyes as she told me of how she relied on her Buddhist practices to get her through a hard time in her life. I could not deny she had experienced much strength when turning to her faith in difficult times, and to her, it was real. I was still thinking about that as she presented an idea that made my head spin.

"I know I can get through anything in this life because I have the Buddha in my heart," she proudly stated.

What? I thought to myself. That's not right. It's Jesus in your heart. That's what all the Bible stories, hymns, and phrases I ever learned proclaimed. You have Jesus in your heart, not Buddha.

"Is something wrong?" She asked, most likely reacting to the perplexed look on my face.

"No. Everything's fine," I replied. "I was just thinking about what you just said about having the Buddha in your heart."

"Yes, I know. It's wonderful." Her eyes misted up again. "I don't know how anybody gets by without help from God."

Even though it was brief, the conversation had a huge impact on me. I was stunned that someone could feel as strongly about their religion as I did mine. Part of me was screaming that it was wrong, but another could not deny that her beliefs were real to her. Until then, I had never met anyone that had the same deep personal connection to their religion as I did to mine. I had to know more.

I spent the next several months reading all I could about theories of Buddhism from as many sources as I could find. Some of my preconceived ideas were confirmed, but I also learned many I hadn't known before. The most significant difference was that I was approaching this study with much more of an open mind. I felt let down by the narrow perceptions of God I had held and was now able to approach this formerly blasphemous material in a different light. It was refreshing and exciting. I never saw the Buddhist woman again. She had only been hired for that one day. I didn't even get her name.

The two most impactful impressions I gleaned from reading about Buddhism was the dedication to love and compassion, which appeared to be the center of the religion. That was the main goal, "Extinguish hurtful behavior and cultivate loving behavior," was a phrase used many times throughout the literature. The other impression was how many similarities there were between Buddhism and Christianity. An excellent book on this is Thich Nhat Hahn's *Living Buddha, Living Christ*. One comparison can be seen in the teachings of Jesus in the Beatitudes and the Five Precepts of Buddhism, both presenting a description of loving behavior.

THE BEATITUDES—MATTHEW 5:3-11

> Blessed are the poor in spirit, for theirs is the kingdom of heaven.
>
> Blessed are those who mourn, for they will be comforted.
>
> Blessed are the meek, for they will inherit the earth.
>
> Blessed are those who hunger and thirst for righteousness, for they will be filled.
>
> Blessed are the merciful, for they will be shown mercy.
>
> Blessed are the pure in heart, for they will see God.
>
> Blessed are the peacemakers, for they will be called sons of God.
>
> Blessed are those who are persecuted because of righteousness, for theirs is the kingdom of heaven.
>
> Blessed are you when people insult you, persecute you and falsely say all kinds of evil against you because of me.

THE FIVE PRECEPTS OF BUDDHISM[1]
Cultivating Compassion
Aware of the suffering caused by the destruction of life, I will cultivate compassion and learn ways to protect the lives of people, animals, plants, and minerals.

Cultivating Loving Kindness
Aware of the suffering caused by exploitation, social injustice, stealing, and oppression, I will cultivate loving-kindness and learn ways to work for the well-being of people, animals, and minerals.

The Oneness of Body and Mind
Aware of the suffering caused by sexual misconduct, I will cultivate responsibility and learn ways to protect the safety and integrity of individuals, couples, families, and society.

Unmindful Speech Can Kill
Aware of the suffering caused by unmindful speech and the inability to listen to others, I will cultivate loving speech and deep listening in order to bring joy and happiness to others and relieve others of their suffering.

Mindful Consuming
Aware of the suffering caused by unmindful consumption, I will cultivate good health, both physical and mental, for myself, my family, and my society by practicing mindful eating, drinking, and consuming.

While I was impressed by the similarities between the two religions, I also felt the pressure of the irreconcilable differences between them. For one, the Plan of Salvation, to a Buddhist, was not needed. There was no need to reconcile oneself before an almighty God. There was no punishment for sins. There was no sins to be forgiven, just hurtful behavior that a person needed to be made aware of and extinguished.

That was a big concept for me to get over. A non-punishing God? No hell? No need for a savior? No need to do anything? This drove right to the heart of my justification that Christianity was the most valid religion. In encounters with others, I always "followed the sin" in discussing, debating, and arguing my beliefs. The way I explained it was that we all sin, and that sin had to be reconciled. Jesus did it on the cross, and that was that.

From my Evangelical perspective, non-Christian religions faltered in this aspect. They could not account for the sin factor, or they were weak on the resolution. That's where I would get them. I said many times, "It is the 'sin transaction' that occurred on the cross that transferred our wrongdoings to Jesus that makes us whole. What about your beliefs?" I knew that whatever they said would not clearly answer the question. Then I had them. Looking back, I cringe when thinking what a jerk I was about the topic.

Another nagging thought I had was about sin, in general. What if sin was not part of the equation? That idea threw me. That and the whole reincarnation thing. Many of the Buddhist teachings say that it takes many lifetimes to reach the pinnacle of loving behavior and achieve "Buddhahood." We always had this nailed with the Hebrews 9:27 verse: "It is destined for a man once to die and then comes judgment." This proved that reincarnation was not real, at least from the Christian perspective. Some astute non-Christian scholars would challenge me, saying that I couldn't prove or disprove any concept from one or two verses in the Bible. Or, that the verse does not specify there is only one life, instead you are judged after each lifetime. In that scenario, judgment was a review as compared with eternal salvation or damnation. Throughout the years, I read more about this topic in *20 Cases Suggestive of Reincarnation*[2] *Many Lives Many Masters*[3], *Journey of the Souls*[4], among others that present their research in a reasonable and balanced way. These books contain many examples of how people have been able to recollect living in another time, place, and body. Several examples provide supporting testimonies and compelling evidence. It's fair to say that after reading about these cases, most people would conclude that reincarnation may not be true for everyone, but it is hard to deny that it occurred with the people in these accounts.

As a result of reading, studying, and talking to scores of people about Buddhism, Eastern philosophy, and reincarnation, I was convinced that other belief systems could be real too, and they could contain at least some aspects of truth. Some of these same truths could also be seen in Christianity, specifically in the teachings of Jesus. This was a breakthrough, and I knew it was a significant departure from my Evangelical roots.

Overall, I was energized to learn more about these new concepts, comparing and contrasting them with ideas I had held close for so many years. At the same time, I could not reconcile some of the ideas that most conflicted with Christianity, such as reincarnation and sin. Nevertheless, I felt I was on to something. The most significant theoretical obstacle was the exclusivist references that Christianity was the only way to God, and outside of that, there was eternal punishment. The familiar verse always shot in my mind when I considered this thought. "I am the way, the truth, the life. No man comes to the father but by me." (John 14:5-6)

While I desperately clung to that verse and others over the years to feel secure in my faith and salvation, these ideas did not fit with other messages of Christianity. An all-loving God who punished people who didn't believe a certain way was beginning to sound inconsistent to me, an idea that I often had. In my younger days, I would suggest, insist, even demand this exclusive way to God was right. In fact, it showed that God was merciful and that we were sinful and stubborn.

The common analogy was of a person with a deadly disease. Suppose someone approaches a sick person with a hypodermic needle containing an antidote guaranteed to cure their illness and restore them to full health. The sick person considers the cure and says, "I do not like needles. I want a pill. If you give me a pill, I will take it and become well."

The doctor replies, "There is no other antidote other than this, and you can have it right now, free of charge. If you do not want it, you will die of your own volition." The ill person curses this cure and tells the doctor to go away. Later they die from their illness. Was it the person bringing the treatment that caused this person's death? No, they did it to themselves. I often used this analogy, emphasizing that no one could say that God does not offer salvation to everyone. You can blame people for being stubborn and dying as a result of their stubbornness. Another version was offering a starving man a sandwich. When he died of starvation because he preferred soup, you couldn't blame the person offering the sandwich. It was the same with God; you couldn't blame Him for people's misfortune if they rejected the only spiritual antidote available to all.

At that time in my life, these scenarios made sense to me and reinforced my Christian beliefs exceptionally well. Importantly, it shifted the blame away from God, which was a good thing. This approach also assumed death was the pending option, but once that was no longer an option, the motivation to avoid damnation vanished as well.

Unfortunately, the enthusiasm of my new-found theological frontier was not shared by my family. Whenever I attempted to explain what I had been learning, questions would come at me like bullets from a Howitzer, especially from Mom and Glenn. "Where did you get this information?" "How do you know it's true if it's not from the Bible?"

I knew all too well that in conservative Christian thinking, considering sources other than the Bible were immediately suspect. Questioning too much could get you into trouble because questioning can raise doubts and doubts erode faith. One way questioning was discouraged was to emphasize that we were to have "simple faith" or "child-like faith." This concept was illustrated by the story where Jesus points to a child and told everyone to have the simple faith and trust just as a child trusts their parents. Exploring complex topics, questioning basic concepts, or spending too much time on contradictory statements were all considered dangerous territory. This idea was certainly exemplified by

X, as he ventured into advanced studies and got all twisted around, and ended up rejecting God, religion, and us.

My encounter with the Buddhist woman and subsequent investigations into Buddhism opened my mind to the idea that God was possibly involved in both of these religions. I recounted many of the other religious beliefs I knew about beyond the Judeo-Christian tradition in which I was raised. For example, Catholicism, Mormonism, Presbyterian, Methodist, Lutheran, Pentecostal, as well as non-Christian religions; Islam, the Spiritual practices of the American Indians, Hindu, and other far eastern religions. As uncomfortable as it was at first, I could not deny there must be something inherently spiritual contained in these beliefs. Most importantly, I would bet that in each of these religious traditions, there were genuinely spiritual people and as well as jerks.

Seeing Godly value in other religions, considering moral guidelines outside of the Bible, and investigating other religious perspectives, was clearly outside of the Bible and especially conservative Christian thinking. I was in uncharted waters. The main difference was that now I did not fear I was going to burn in hell or be rejected by God.

When talking to my mother about my new perspectives on religion, I sensed her deep concern and could tell she was disturbed by listening to my ideas. I told her I felt as if I was the first person to sail off in the ocean toward the horizon when people believed the Earth was flat.

"Everyone is warning me that I am going to fall off the edge to a miserable death," I said. "I'm here to say that I've been past the horizon and back, and it's okay. I'm okay, Mom! I'm not going to burn in hell; I'm just not!"

In turning this over and over in my mind, I concluded that if spirituality and religion were two separate concepts, and people could experience spiritual connections to God in many ways then:

Lesson 3 — There are many ways to God.

Research related to this can be found in the psychology of religion. Areas of interest in this discipline explore how people gravitate to specific religions out of the 4,500 organized religious groups around the world. One researcher, psychologist Steven Reiss, published a book in 2015 titled *The 16 Strivings for God,* where he describes how people select the religion that aligns with their specific desires.[5] In his research, he surveyed 7,700 people from diverse backgrounds to better understand common motivational factors and desires. His research showed that people have sixteen basic desires based on their individual psychological needs. He then conducted further analysis to identify correlations to religion. While he admittedly was biased to the Judeo-Christian image of God, his work points out that humans have psychological needs, and many choose specific religions that align with those needs.

16 BASIC DESIRES

Acceptance – the desire for positive self-regard

Curiosity – the desire for understanding

Eating – the desire for food

Family – the desire to raise children and spend time with siblings

Honor – the desire for upright character

Idealism – the desire for social justice

Independence – the desire for self-reliance

Order – the desire for structure

Physical activity – the desire for exercise

Power – the desire for influence or leadership

Romance – the desire for beauty and sex

Saving – the desire to collect

Social Contact – the desire to have fun with peers

Status – the desire for respect based on social standing

Tranquility – the desire for safety

Vengeance – the desire to confront provocations

Two thoughts came to mind as I read through Reiss's work. The first was there were probably people that thought the idea of someone picking their religion to fulfill basic psychological needs was blasphemous. According to Reiss's framework, my perception of God fulfilled my needs for *acceptance, curiosity, order,* and *tranquility*. The second thought was even more severe; the idea that God was made in the image of man.

At this point in my journey, I knew I was rejecting core beliefs years in development. I noticed, too, that my nagging thoughts grew in frequency and the level of discomfort as well. I wondered why this was happening and found answers in a relatively simple concept.

CONTRARY TO ... YOUR OWN BELIEFS

The tension caused by differences between my religious beliefs and my internal beliefs grew to the point I could not ignore them any longer. After the talk with the Buddhist woman, I began noticing the conflict mostly when I was explaining that Jesus was the only way to God. I knew the theology inside and out, but at times I was bothered by the words I said.

Living with internal tension is a common experience for many. For example, people who work at jobs they dislike or stay in unhappy relationships experience the tension of wanting one thing while struggling to make a needed change. In these situations, people hold their inconsistent feelings in check, sometimes for their entire lives.

The term describing the tension between beliefs is "cognitive dissonance." This is a situation when a person experiences tension, or dissonance, when considering conflicting ideas, or cognitions. One well-known example is the buyer's remorse scenario. Suppose someone is looking to buy a car. They conduct some research, go to the dealer, and sign the papers for their new wheels. When they tell their friend they purchased a car, and the friend suggests another car is safer or more economical, internal tension rises as the buyer considers this new information right after they have committed to buying the new vehicle.

An interesting point is if a person perceives a high amount of pressure to maintain their beliefs, then are presented with a competing idea, they experience lower levels of dissonance. Conversely, if a person perceives low pressure to change, they will experience a higher level of dissonance as they struggle to decide what to do. In another car example, suppose a couple is going used car shopping with a maximum budget of $25,000. When the salesperson shows them a top-line sedan that costs $75,000, they easily turn it down easily because it dramatically exceeds their budget, low dissonance. When they are shown a new, lower-priced car for $27,000, they experience dissonance because they didn't think they would be able to buy a new car, and it only exceeds their maximum budget slightly.

The level of tension a person can tolerate depends on the individual. Some people can live with it for years, going to a job they hate, remaining in an abusive relationship, or participating in religious rituals they find meaningless. For others, the moment they are unhappy, they immediately address the issue.

When thinking about religion, many people are frightened of other belief systems because they cannot cope with the uncomfortable feelings of doubt. Certainly, thoughts of eternal damnation and torture will minimize dissonant feelings of competing religious beliefs held by conservative Christians.

Dissonant feelings are generally reduced in three ways.[1] The first is to simply change the attitude about what is being resisted. In the example of the car purchase, the purchaser could go back to the dealer and get out of the deal and purchase a different car.

The second way people reduce negative feelings is to seek out information that supports one of the two conflicting ideas. In this way, a person obtains sufficient evidence to alleviate the tension of conflicting concepts. An example of this is a new mom who believes breastfeeding is healthy and is told by her parents that breastfeeding is not good. Feeling uncomfortable that her parents are opposed to breastfeeding, the new mother experiences dissonant feelings. After researching several articles on the subject, she finds that reputable physicians clearly endorse nursing. The new mother's dissonance is reduced because her position is supported.

The third and most common way people alleviate dissonant feelings is to trivialize the conflicting attitudes or behaviors. A typical example of this would be a high school student being asked to go to the movies with his friends the night before an important test. Feeling the tension between the two choices, the student reasons that it may not be an important test, or that his average in the class was high and that a low grade on this test would not endanger his overall grade. Deciding the test is not that important; he trivializes the conflicting attitude and enjoys the evening with his friends.

My dissonant feeling increased when I began doubting the judgment and damnation messages of the Plan of Salvation. I resolved the dissonance by backing off the fear-based theology, changing my attitude, and investigating other belief systems.

Sometimes when I talk with people who hold the rigid Christian beliefs I once clung to, I play with them by posing questions clearly pointing out the disparity of their beliefs. For example, I might ask, "What is better for a child, to be raised in an angry, abusive heterosexual Christian home, or in a home with two loving and committed homosexuals that have no religious affiliation?" The responses I get most of the time is generally silence, with the person blinking a lot and shifting in their seat.

For those who are not one hundred percent comfortable with their religion or spiritual journey, it is essential to understand the source of your dissonant feelings. By working through our doubts and feelings to better understand what we believe and why we will be able to see our own bias and free ourselves to change.

Lesson 4 — When we understand our conflicting feelings, we can free ourselves to change.

This was an important point in time for me because it helped me reconcile my many nagging thoughts about my beliefs, as well as how to handle these uncomfortable feelings. This allowed me to separate myself from my long-held beliefs. After that, I felt free to investigate other perspectives of God and spirituality without fear. I knew now that God was bigger than any religion or theology, with no group having a complete grasp of God.

However, in considering this, I began to wonder, how do we know anything about God? Certainly, most of the world's religions were based on ancient books. We also learn through spiritual leaders and teachers. Some have seen visons or claim to have heard directly from God. The question for me was: how can anyone know for sure? In fact, how do we know anything?

HOW DO WE KNOW ANYTHING?

How do we know anything? I came across this topic in my studies as a general question about the nature of learning. It certainly is a question that directly relates to our understanding of God. Often starting as young children, we build our concepts of God from many sources throughout our lives. But how do we *know* anything? Many theories and models of how we acquire knowledge are covered in the field of *epistemology*, meaning, the theory of knowledge. One popular model of knowing is comprised of four perspectives and was introduced by Charles Pierce in 1887.[1]

The first way is by *authority*. This is best described as the only way we learn as a child. This happens mainly with our parents, teachers, and religious leaders. We accept what they say simply and only because they are authority figures. There is no verification, no validation. As children, whatever an authority figure says, we believe it's true.

The second way we know things is through *tenacity*. This is the assurance we give ourselves that once we know something to be true, if new information is presented to the contrary, what we believe remains. Prejudice falls into this category. My struggle with conservative Christian beliefs, family, and friends is an indication of a strong, tenacious level of knowing. Certainly, tenacity was an important component of my beliefs, fueled by the idea that bad things would happen if you doubted or questioned the Plan of Salvation.

The third way we know things is through *a priori* beliefs. This knowing occurs without any direct evidence. Intuition is an excellent example of this type of knowledge. Sometimes you just know something. When someone asks, "How can you be so sure?" The answer usually is, "I don't know why I just am." The idea of women's intuition usually referrers to an uncanny ability of women to know what is happening or what is about to occur without any concrete information.

The fourth way of knowing is through *scientific investigation*. This specifically refers to empirical science, meaning that knowledge is gained through observation. An example is of boiling water. A teacher tells us that water boils at 212 degrees Fahrenheit. That is authority. Scientific investigation is obtained when you stick a thermometer into a pot of water, turn on the heat, and observe that it starts to boil at 212 degrees.

While generally considered the most reliable form of knowing, scientific investigation has one limitation. This is that any change must be observable; meaning changes in whatever situation being studied must be able to be seen or measured. The observable change for the boiling water experiment is bubbles of air forming in the water, and the measurement is the temperature. The reason why this can be considered a limitation is that great care must be taken to identify what the expected change will be, in addition to how exactly it will be measured. Otherwise, the scientific conclusion will be considered faulty and inaccurate.

The four ways of knowing can also be applied to our understanding of God and spiritual topics. We all initially learn about God from authority figures. Tenacious beliefs about God are often grounded in our upbringing and solidified with positive experiences of religious traditions, holiday celebrations, and even mystical experiences. Also, the level of tenacious knowing can be enhanced, as mentioned earlier, by theological beliefs stating that doubting a particular belief may be the ticket to an eternity of pain and suffering.

As you might guess, scientific knowing about God and spiritual topics can be controversial. Nevertheless, scores of researchers have been investigating spiritual topics in scientific settings for centuries. The topics investigated have ranged from attempts to "prove" of the existence of God, to laboratory settings measuring the effects of prayer on plants, microorganisms, and physical objects. The same scientific challenges come into play with these experiments as with any other. What exactly is being studied? How is it being defined and measured? What are the factors affecting any changes? What factors could be confounding the results?

A priori knowledge of God can be experienced in many ways. The quiet assurance from reading scriptures or singing hymns, and, the "still small voice" in times of need, are a few examples. Although I didn't realize it at the time, it was the intuitive assurance of the born-again Christians in their relationship to God that I initially so desperately wanted. How could they have been so sure? I wondered. The mystical experience was the a priori validation I needed to say that I was born again and to be considered a Christian. Interestingly, it was my intuitive nagging thoughts about the judgmental and conditional love of God that hurled me out of organized religion.

People who claim they heard or saw God fuels their commitment to stay close to their chosen traditions and sacred books. This raised a multitude of questions for me. The holy men and women inspired by God to write the scriptures that have been studied for years had to be correct. Right? If this is true, then knowledge about God must be solely based on authority. If so, who were these writers? Did they get it right? I knew of some cultural influences in their writings. Were there other influences? What about the inconsistencies and errors within the scriptures? More so, what about all the different religions whose sacred texts describe God in many different and seemingly incompatible ways?

This was when I realized the basis for any religious belief ultimately comes down to a priori belief. There is no way for anyone to objectively know about or prove God exists, let alone understand how we should relate to him or her, or verify that my sins were transferred out of my account, or any other specific religious tenets. Some would even say that a priori belief is the most significant component in believing anything, even in our physical universe.

Understanding that knowledge can come from several sources and that knowing is a subjective term, I was able to free myself to look for God outside of the limits of sacred documents and organized religion. Then I began to see God everywhere.

Lesson 5 — It is important to understand how you have decided what you believe is true.

PRAYER— THE SEQUEL

For me, prayer was always a central part of my faith, but also a journey into the unknown. As a child, my efforts began with asking Jesus to "be near" and "bless everybody," and then expanding my scope to reciting a laundry list of things I wanted, including the infamous electric car. When I was in the born-again phase of my journey, I felt I had a special relationship with God. I could venture into the Holy of Holies just as the Old Testament High Priests did, to spend time with the Almighty. While I felt closer to God during those times, I couldn't figure out how to pray and see the results I wanted. My prayers had changed from wanting things to wanting direction and clarity in decision making. These requests were related to picking what college to attend, or my first job. These requests were not clearly answered. The best I could say was that the decisions were "obvious" to me at the time, which was what I prayed for, but I guess I was looking for something more dramatic. Certainly, my doubts about prayer expanded exponentially when prayers offered during the time my life was imploding went unanswered.

As always, my inner compulsion to know how prayer worked, if it did at all, drove me to spend some time studying the topic in grad school. The first step in this investigation was to see how prayer affected those who prayed, not for others, but themselves. This is known as inward prayer.

INWARD PRAYER

It is important to note that much of the research involving inward prayer can be seen in the reviews of religion and health, specifically religious behavior and health. This is because the behavioral aspects of religion (e.g., church attendance, frequency of prayer, or reading of sacred texts) are seen as being a component of religiosity. However, my interests were in a smaller number of studies that centered on the effectiveness of inward prayer as a single factor.

Reviews of 35 studies specifically addressing inward prayer and health included a total participant population of 9,435 and addressed a variety of health-related issues such as pain management[1], pulmonary disease[2], length of sobriety[3], pregnancy[4], and Leukemia[5], among others. Although the number of studies and participants may seem considerable, it is essential to note that these 35 studies occurred over almost 50 years and can be considered scarce. The author of one review, Dr. Michael McCullough from Southern Methodist University, suggests that the low number of studies exist because a) scholars do not believe it works, b) others do not want to "put God to the test," and c) limited theoretical definitions make empirical studies difficult.

Furthermore, the author of this review pointed out that the Judeo-Christian Bible teaches that not all prayer works, with some conditions reported to worsen as a result of prayer. For example, the Old Testament story of King David and his son, who was critically ill.[6] King David fasted, prayed, and pleaded with God to spare his child, but seven days later, the child died. When David was told his child was dead, he washed, changed his clothes, and ate. His servants questioned his behavior and asked him how he was able to fast, pray, and plead for his child while alive, and now return to a normal life.

He answered, "While the child was still alive, I fasted and wept. I thought, 'Who knows? The Lord may be gracious to me and let the child live.' But now that he is dead, why should I fast? Can I bring him back again? I will go to him, but he will not return to me."

McCullough explains circumstances may deteriorate even in times of prayer "if persons are led through times of repentance, trial, or 'dark nights of the soul'" as a part of a growing or maturing process.[7]

In studying the results of inward prayer research, the data indicate positive responses in measures of subjective well-being, coping, and psychiatric symptoms. It is essential to note in many of the studies, gender, health, life events, socioeconomic status were not accounted for, and may have impacted the results. As McCullough concluded, "As with most research on prayer and health, uncontrolled confounds compromise the validity of any conclusions."[7]

Interestingly, in a review of prayer research conducted in 2016, 20 years after McCullough published his findings, researchers could only state that prayer "seems to help patients to cope in times of illness and crisis." They continued that more prayer research is needed to determine the impact on patients but can be recommended as part of a holistic approach to health.[8]

This was an interesting review and aligned with my conclusions. However, I had more questions. What about praying for others? In the churches and groups, I attended, there were countless requests for prayer for people who were sick or in need. This was the next stop in my prayer research.

PRAYING FOR OTHERS—THE RESULTS

Many times, when I prayed for someone or heard others say someone needed prayer, I often wondered if these efforts had any effect. During my doctoral work, I spent several months researching this topic and learned about seven important studies. The earliest study into the effectiveness of praying for others, or intercessory prayer, was conducted by the Englishman, Francis Galton (1872), and published in his article "Statistical Inquiries into the Efficacy of Prayer."[1] In this report, the author studied the data of life expectancy of clergy and members of the royal houses. These groups were assumed to pray more than the general population and to be supported more through intercessory prayer than anyone else. However, the study results indicated the opposite, with physicians and lawyers outlasting clergy, and missionaries not living any longer than commoners.

The problem with his study was that the only difference between the groups was the assumed amount of prayer experienced by the clergy, resulting in conclusions that prayer is ineffective. Nevertheless, it was an attempt and a starting point in the study of this phenomenon.

The next study of intercessory prayer was conducted in 1965, with 48 patients suffering from progressively deteriorating psychological or rheumatic diseases in a London Hospital.[2] The patients were not told they were in any type of study. Prayer groups were assigned to pray for the patients daily for six months. The results showed no significant difference between the two groups. The authors stated that the low number of participants might not have been sufficient enough to detect any differences.

Another study followed four years later in the United States with leukemic children.[3] In this study, ten children with severe leukemia were prayed for daily by families of a Protestant church, while eight similar children were not prayed for, and neither group was told they were in a study. After 15 months, the mortality rates of the experimental group was 30%, and the mortality rate of the control group was 75%. While the results looked positive, other than the small sample, a significant flaw was that the participants were not matched for the severity of condition. As a result, biological factors may have had a significant effect on the outcomes.

One hundred and sixteen years after Galton published his work, results from a highly publicized prayer study involving humans was presented by Randolph Byrd from the University of California at San Francisco.[4] This study was conducted with 393 coronary care unit patients to determine if intercessory prayer to the Judeo-Christian God had any effect on hospitalized patients. All participants involved, including the hospital staff, knew a study on the impact of prayer was being conducted, though no one knew who was receiving prayers. The intercessors were asked to pray daily for a rapid recovery and prevention of complications and death in the patient.[5]

The results showed the group receiving prayers had a better outcome. The authors summarized that even though prayer by others outside of the study, personal prayer, and strength of religious convictions were not accounted for, "Based on these data, there seemed to be an effect, and that effect was presumed to be beneficial."[6]

Ten years later, a follow-up study was conducted with 999 cardiac patients in a critical care unit of a Kansas City, MO hospital.[7] The purpose was to determine whether intercessory prayer reduced adverse effects and length of stay for these patients. The results showed an overall decrease in adverse outcomes with no difference in length of stays.

Another study conducted regarding the effects of intercessory prayer examined the healing effects using a population of 40 patients with advanced acquired immunodeficiency syndrome (AIDS).[8] The people providing treatment, called "healers" in this study, were from mixed theistic and non-theistic traditions including Christian and Jewish intercessors, Buddhist, Native-American, Shamanic, graduates from schools of bioenergy, and meditative healing. The healers were given participants on a random and rotating basis for a 10-week period. Each participant was treated by a total of 10 different healers for one hour a day, six days per week. The results showed that the 20 patients experienced positive results on 6 of the 11 outcome measures; significantly fewer outpatient doctor visits, hospitalizations, days of hospitalization, new occurrences of disease, reported lower illness severity levels, and increased levels of mood.

The authors concluded that their studies showed the positive influence of distant healing and urged additional research to be conducted to understand how it works in general, as well as in other health-related applications.

Finally, the findings of the most extensive intercessory prayer study ever conducted was published in late 2006. This was a multi-million dollar study funded by the Templeton Foundation titled "Study of the Therapeutic Effects of Intercessory Prayer (STEP) in Cardiac Bypass Patients – A Multi-Center Randomized Trial of Uncertainty and Certainty of Receiving Intercessory Prayer."[9] The lead researcher was the renowned Herbert Benson, MD of the Mind/Body Medical Institute, affiliated with Harvard Medical School in Boston. The goal of the study was to observe if intercessory prayer, or the knowledge of it, would affect recovery after bypass surgery. The participants totaled 1,802 with three groups of 1) 604 receiving prayers after being told that they may or may not be prayed for 2) 597 not receiving prayers after being told that they may or may not receive prayers, and 3) 601 receiving prayer after being told they would receive prayers.

The agents agreed to pray for 14 days using the standard phrase for the participant to have "a successful surgery with a quick, healthy recovery and no complications."

Results showed both groups that were told they may or may not receive prayers, with approximately half receiving prayers, had almost the same percentage of complications (51 and 52%). Interestingly, the group that was told they were going to receive prayers and received them had the highest number of complications (59%).

Overall, these studies indicate supplementary intercessory prayer can show no results, or significant improvement, or increased negative results.

One area I was interested in studying was what impact of praying for others has on the people conducting the prayers. This is called the agent effect, and it was a part of my dissertation.

My study was designed to measure the impact of praying or meditating for others on a person's quality of life (QOL).[10] To measure QOL, a validated survey was used that provided ten subscale scores. The agents filled out the survey at the beginning of the study to obtain a baseline QOL score and were provided a target person's first name, last name initial, city, and state. The agents were asked to pray or meditate daily for their target person's general health and well being. Specific thoughts and amount of time spent was up to them. After four weeks, the agents were given the same survey again to observe any changes in their scores.

At the conclusion of the study, significant improvements were seen in 8 out of 10 subscale scores in the QOL survey in the agents. The areas of improvement were seen in vitality and decreased bodily pain scores. Other trends of improvement were seen in general health and restrictions as a result of emotional problems.

Spending time reviewing prayer studies was important to me because I was wondering how we can navigate through our lives. I considered prayer almost a separate topic from theology and religion and was aware that it had been studied for many years.

My conclusion, after reviewing hundreds of prayer studies for my dissertation, was that, in general, they showed barely significant positive results. A little disappointing, but notable.

One last area to investigate related to prayer I learned about started with my conversation with the Buddhist women. Initially, it was an afterthought, but I was surprised to find a host of research had been conducted on the impact of meditation.

MEDITATION— A COMMON GROUND

Many books, videos, recordings, and cell phone apps are available to provide instruction on a variety of meditation practices. It's easy to be confused and unsure about where to start. One reason for this is that our western culture does not have much to offer regarding meditation. We are aware of only a few states of consciousness; sleeping, waking, daydreaming, and Spring Break. Religious and spiritual groups in eastern culture have been exploring states of consciousness for thousands of years.

Initially, in my journey as a young born-again Christian, I kept a distance from the topic of meditation. The Evangelical Christians, in general, shy away from this because meditation is not mentioned to any substantial degree in the Bible, and because it has strong ties to eastern religious practices. This resistance was demonstrated in hundreds of conversations with my mom after I moved away from Evangelical Christianity and organized religion.

"Do you go to church regularly?" Mom asked.

"No."

"Why not?" she replied, squinting at me.

"Because God is right here with us now, he is not contained in a building."

"Do you pray?" she asked, continuing the interrogation.

"Yes, I pray. I've also been trying different types of meditation."

"What do you mean, meditation?" Her brow furrowed, expressing even more skepticism.

"Quieting my mind, listening to soft music."

"So, you're a Buddhist now? That's not good," she shot back in an accusatory tone.

"No, Mom, I'm not a Buddhist," I answered, trying to calm her.

"Do you read the Bible?" She continued the line of questioning.

"Yes."

"Good, okay. I'll stop with the questions for now," she concluded with a smile.

The most common method in meditation is concentrating on breathing. Our minds cannot focus on two things at once, so if we focus on our breath, we cannot focus on any other thought. Even people who proudly state they are excellent multitaskers are shifting between two or more subjects very quickly, not simultaneously. Typical meditation exercises suggest taking a long breath in for a count of four, and to breathe out for the same count. Other methods direct people to breathe in and out for a count of one, then continue with two, up to a ten count, and back down to one. If you break your concentration at any point, you start over again at one until you can complete the full sequence without breaking your concentration.

As I explored different types of meditation exercises, I quickly saw the benefits. I could feel how it calmed me, especially if I was angry or experiencing stress. After maintaining a regular practice of meditation, I was able to concentrate better at work and on other projects and tasks. Fascinated by these results, and driven by my innate curiosity, I had to learn more. I used my time in graduate school to review the research around this ancient practice.

The goal of most meditation is the control of brain activity leading to quietness and calming, which positively impacts nervous and physiologic systems. Common elements contained in all varieties of meditation are to increase awareness and bring the mind under conscious control. Individual practices vary regarding the specific imagery, breathing techniques, attentional strategies, and specific goal attributes used, such as increased generosity, love, compassion, or wisdom. Meditative practices to this depth are not usually found in our western culture. However, some forms of meditation are growing in popularity in our culture and being used in stress management, relaxation, and self-confidence. More intense forms of meditation, called concentration or insight meditation, focus on examining the nature of the mind, consciousness, and expanded awareness.

Many studies with meditation have shown positive results in the treatment of anxiety, social phobia, bronchial asthma, insomnia, reduction of high blood pressure, drug and alcohol abuse, and myocardial infarction, among others. Changes of neural and physiological activities is thought to be accomplished through the use of imagery, calming, and quieting techniques.

Researchers at Harvard Medical School have also studied the impact of meditation. Led by Dr. Herbert Benson, this group identified a meditative state as the Relaxation Response (RR). This is when a person repeats a word, sound, prayer, thought, phrase, or muscular activity, resulting in breaking the normal train of thought. Their studies showed significant reductions in hypertension, cardiac arrhythmias, chronic pain, anxiety, and depression.[1]

In my research on meditation. I learned about a specific practice called *Vipassana Meditation,* which means to "see things as they really are." This approach was developed in India by Siddhattha Gotama more than 2500 years ago. Siddhattha developed a ten-day sequence of activities to promote self-transformation through self-observation. It focuses on the deep interconnection between the mind and body. The method was presented as a "universal remedy for universal ills." Siddhattha used this technique to become "enlightened" and thus became Gotama Budda, the first Buddha.

Vipassana centers can be found around the world, teaching the same ten-day program used by Gotama. I found one in Shelburne Falls, Massachusetts and put it on the top of my list of things to do. I soon realized that while the courses are ten-days in length, participants are required to arrive one day in advance. This, plus travel back home, meant I needed a total of twelve days to attend the program. It took me eight years before my schedule was clear for the block of time required, and I was able to accrue the vacation time. I booked a session one summer in late August.

The first three days of the session were one of the hardest experiences I ever endured. We spent about nine hours a day in a large room, or Dharma Hall, sitting on meditation mats, eyes closed. At times, we received direction on what to concentrate on from the leaders at the front of the room. We had breaks for meals and personal time to walk around the grounds or rest in our rooms. A required component for all participants is to take a vow of "Noble Silence." This means the participant could not bring any reading or writing materials, cell phones, or computers. Eye contact and speaking with others is also prohibited. The purpose of invoking Nobel Silence is to help participants be alone with their thoughts in order to achieve the full benefit of the course. After the initial shock of literally no mental activity, I observed my mind slowing and relaxing significantly after day four. Without the deluge of TV, radio, phone, reading, and writing, the pace of the mind slows, but it was an excruciating process for the first few days. However, at the end of the ten days I felt much more emotionally grounded and had a newfound ability to concentrate more deeply and longer than ever before. The feeling for me was as if I had been treading water for some time, and was finally able to touch bottom.

Engaging in meditation consistently has had the most profound impact on me than any other spiritual or religious experience, practice, or activity. I know when I am upset, angry, lost, or in need of solace, I can retreat to one or a combination of meditation practices to be restored to a good place once again.

The fascinating aspect of meditation is in its simplicity. Concentrating on breathing, quieting the mind, and mindfulness is the goal. There are no theological or religious requirements in order to engage in this activity and reap the benefits. Anyone in any religion or belief system can participate in one of the many forms of meditation. It is very much . . . a common ground.

Lesson 6 — Meditation is a powerful and effective way to experience peace and the presence of God. It is universal, transcending all bounds of religion, theology, and belief systems.

THE GAME CHANGER— A CONVERSATION WITH GOD

I was in my mid-forties, finishing my graduate studies, and writing up my dissertation on the impact of prayer and meditation when it happened. At that time, I was comfortable distancing myself from conservative Christianity and investigating other religions. I had many discussions with my Buddhist friends, as well as my Muslim, and Hindu friends, learning much about the world's largest religions. It was then I stumbled on to something that upended all my thinking.

It was a beautiful summer day with puffy cumulus clouds marching in slow procession in a deep blue sky. I met a woman through friends, and we started dating. We were heading back from a weekend in Rhode Island and decided to take a detour north on a winding highway along the Connecticut River. Only able to see glimpses of the river, we turned off on the road to a town we hoped was on the water. Sure enough, we drove into a quaint old town right on the river, complete with old churches, a town square, and a two-block shopping area. The buildings were no more than three stories high and decorated with the millwork typical of New England homes in the early nineteen hundreds. Signs were pointing to scenic this and historic that were posted everywhere. We parked and began a slow walk down the streets, a warm breeze wafted through the trees, while birds flittered happily about, seeming to enjoy the summer as much as we were.

Years ago, the center of town had apparently contained residences and businesses alike, although they now had all been converted to storefront establishments. A mixture of antique stores, knick-knack shops, clothing stores, and galleries now opened their doors to attract those wandering through the town. Fully in character, my girlfriend wanted to investigate each store. Being an "avid shopper" does not nearly describe the intensity and voracity of her shopping acumen. As we headed to the first store, I took a quick inventory of the number of shops ahead of us, probably two dozen. Admittedly not my favorite pastime, I wanted to make the best of the day for both of us so I decided I would go along and wander for as long as I could. The frustration of the step-by-step and rack-by-rack detailed search was compounded a zillion times because my experience taught me there was a 100% chance the excursion would end with not one purchase. Not one.

Nodding in approval saying, "Yes, that is a lovely thimble," or "that antique fork would make a wonderful

ANGEL IN TRAINING

place setting, I wonder where the other 99 pieces are?" I headed for the door, as usual, to walk around a little, waiting for my beloved to finish her inventory sweep. I noticed a bookstore next door and ventured in. This was obviously an old home at one point, with low ceilings, several small adjoining rooms, and squeaky wooden floors. Looking through the bookshelves, I found the psychology section, then the religion section, my typical stops.

I was about to leave when my eye caught a book that seemed familiar titled *Conversations with God: An uncommon dialogue* by Neal Donald Walsch.[1] I remembered it was on the New York Times bestseller list not too long before. My only recollection of it had been that it was some sort of a pop-psychology book on religion, so I wasn't too interested. But I now had some time to kill since my significant other was only on shop two of many.

As I began to read the first pages, I was surprised to learn the book was about a conversation with God. "Yeah, right," I thought, recalling the mass suicide of the 913 followers of Jim Jones in Guyana in 1978, the Heaven's Gate cult deaths during Hale-Bopp comet in 1997, and how dangerous it could be to believe people who heard the voice of God. Nevertheless, I read on. Surprisingly, Walsch's story kept my attention as he described his experience.

Over several years, Walsch kept a note pad handy in order to record his thoughts and ideas. It sounded as if it was a form of venting and emotional release for him. It appeared he needed it too. He was frustrated with life, relationships, and work. One night he was in a typical frustrated mood and began to write. Except for this time, something else took over the writing. He described it as something took control over his hand, and the words came from somewhere other than him, providing dictation. He was surprised and skeptical at first, but then he relinquished to the process and continued to write. This process resulted in the production of over 21 books over several years and a world-wide foundation offering work groups, study groups, conferences, and lectures. The first book focused on individuals; the second on the community, and the third on universal truths and perspectives. The other books discuss both general and specific topics related to life, love, health, wealth, and death, in fascinating detail.

As I read through book one in the store, I appreciated his demeanor and attitude. He stated several times that he did not initially believe this was a conversation with God, that he even questioned his own thoughts and actions during the whole process. I found comfort in not focusing on where the words came from and why he of all people received these "messages," but weighed the ideas on their own merit, whatever the source may be. He clearly leaves the decision up to the reader to believe or not believe, or to accept or reject the ideas presented in the texts.

This was an important point for me. Just think of all the religions and religious leaders that proclaim they have "The Truth" and that we *must* believe them and join with them or else face the consequences. Certainly, that was what I learned during my Evangelical Christian days, and unfortunately, I was good at conveying that message exceptionally well.

Walsch emphasizes that no one has to, should, or must believe anything he has written. A theme throughout the material is that there is nothing that we should, ought, or must do, or not do. We decide our actions based on the outcomes we want to see.

This material and its origin speak directly to the issue of the validity of the sacred texts of the world's largest religions and how God has communicated with us throughout history. The *Conversations with God* (CwG) material address this topic in-depth throughout the books and includes a detailed discussion in the book, *The New Revelations: A Conversation with God.*[2] Walsch points out the tendency for people throughout history to relegate God's words to ancient texts only. This idea spoke to me as it was something I had often wondered about over the years. Why would God stop communicating? Wouldn't God have something to say to humankind, to his creation, in the last few thousand years? Some sort of reminder, clarification, or application, perhaps? But then I would always revert to what I had been taught and defend the authenticity of the Biblical texts. If these discussions arose, I started with the two New Testament verses:

Matthew 5:18- I tell you the truth, until heaven and Earth disappear, not the least stroke of a pen, will by any means disappear from the Law until everything is accomplished.

And the second, more ominous verse;

> Revelation 22:18- I warn everyone who hears the words of the prophecy of this book: If anyone adds anything to them, God will add to him plagues described. And if anyone takes words away from this book of prophecy, God will take away from him his share in the tree of life and in the holy city, which are described in this book.

There it was again, the ultimatum used for millennia. Believe this or bear the consequences. At that time, I would go into all the proof texts of the authenticity of the scriptures and how they are reliable Words of God, review the oral tradition, the Dead Sea Scrolls, etc. But what about the sacred books of two of the world's other most popular religions like Hinduism and Islam? Certainly, they had something to offer, even though they contradict each other at the most basic levels. And what about these writings by Walsch? Are these valid? I received an answer in a provocative dialog in *The New Revelations* text where Walsch brings up the matter of scripture validity. I have reproduced it here, beginning with Walsch's question of why anyone would want to read *The New Revelations* book. (The author's questions are in bolded type and the responses follow.)

> **Why would I want to read this book when I've already been told by True Believers that all the answers are in the other books?**
>
> Because you have not heeded them.
>
> **Yes, we have. We believe we have.**
>
> That's why you now need help. You believe you have, but you have not.
>
> You keep saying that your Holy Book (your cultures have many different ones) is what has given you the authority to treat each other the way you are treating each other, to do what you are doing.
>
> You are able to say that only because you have not really listened to the deeper message of

these books. You have read them, but you have not really *listened* to them.

But we *have*. We are doing what they *say* we should be doing!

No. You are doing what YOU say that they say you should be doing.

What does that mean?

It means that the basic message of all the sacred scriptures is the same. What is different is how human beings have been interpreting them.

There is nothing "wrong" with having different interpretations. What may not benefit you, however, is separating yourself over these differences, and killing each other as a result of these differences.

That is what you are now doing.

It is what you have been doing for quite some time.

You cannot agree even within a particular group of you, much less between groups, about what a particular book says and what it means, and you use these disagreements as justification for slaughter.

You argue among yourselves about what the Qur'an says, and about what its words mean. You argue among yourselves about what the Bible says, and what its words mean. You argue among yourselves about what the Veda says, what the Bhagavad-Gita says, what the Lun-yu says, what the Pali Canon says, what the Tao-te Ching says, what the Talmud says, what the Hadith says, what the Book of Mormon says...

And what of the Upanishad, the I Ching, the Adi Granth, the Mahabharata, the Kojiki?

Okay, we get the point.

No, actually, you don't. And *that's* the point. The point is, there are *many* holy writings and sacred scriptures, and you act as if there is only one.

It is *your* sacred scripture that is *really* sacred. All the rest are poor substitutes at best, and blasphemies at worst.

Not only is there only one Sacred Scripture, there is also one way to *interpret* that Scripture: your way.

This spiritual arrogance is what has caused you your greatest sorrow as a species. You have suffered more—and caused *other* people to suffer more—over your ideas about God that over your ideas about anything else in the human experience.

You have turned the source of the greatest joy into the source of greatest pain.[3]

I was dismayed, thinking that if everyone just went ahead and believed anything they wanted, then the world would be in chaos with people fighting over who was right and who was wrong. The people or religion with the most power and money would be the winners. Interestingly, Walsch points out that is exactly what is happening now:

> Your present beliefs are turning your world upside-down. And inside-out. You are tearing yourselves apart, blowing yourselves up, ripping yourselves to pieces, pulling yourselves in every direction, poisoning yourselves with your beliefs. Your present beliefs are not supporting you; they are killing you.[4]

I read as much of the book as I could that day in the store and bought that copy. Eventually, I bought the entire series and have them on my bookshelf at home. As I read through the CwG books, some of the ideas were strange to me, and, at first, I didn't know what to make of them, but many of them rang true and resonated with my innermost feelings. Whatever the term was, I had a sense of familiarity with this information that seemed not only to make sense but in many cases to verbalize what I had thought for years.

I am not going to review all the CwG concepts and ideas here. I invite you to read all or any of the CwG books or go to their web site (listed in the Suggested Readings and Resources in the back of this book) to learn about the CwG material. However, in my journey, these ideas had an enormous impact on me and my beliefs, some of which I will share here.

The crucial point for me was to lay to rest the idea of the punishing and punitive God. I had already come to this conclusion, but these readings helped me to solidify and expand on the concept. It was one of the first nagging thoughts about God I had growing up and all through my conservative Christian years. The idea of God being both loving creator and sustainer of hell just didn't make sense.

Even when I presented the standard line, "I know it sounds harsh, but that's what the Bible says," I didn't totally believe it. Nevertheless, I continued to recite the verses that said all sinners would be punished except the True Believers.

Another idea I had struggled with is that if God is all-powerful, then he would not need anything or want anything; therefore, he does not demand anything from us. In the CwG texts, Walsch says that if God demanded anything, it would mean he needed something and therefore was lacking or incomplete in some way. In that light, the whole sin/redemption scenario comes into question. Needless to say, this is a major tenant of all of Christendom and could be unsettling for many. Still, it sounded true to me. For example, if a person had all the money in the world, why would they need more?

I discussed this new-found perspective with a friend of mine who was also a conservative Christian. He responded that God created humankind and our propensity to sin, not because he needed to do it, or because he was a mean and insecure deity. It was because he wanted to do it. He agreed God was all-powerful and did not need anything, but added that he created us for his pleasure. But to me, needing and wanting can be close in meaning. Something seemed lacking and incomplete in either case. After thinking about this for a while, even if this conventional definition of God did not portray Him as a mean deity, it at least portrayed Him as a cruel prankster. In this perspective, God created the Garden of Eden then placed Adam and Eve in it, telling them to not eat of the tree of the knowledge of good and evil. Knowing that Adam would falter, God waited for the apple to be eaten and then, bam, that was it, they were banished out of the garden, and the rest is history. And all this was for God's pleasure? That is a strange type of love, and I could no longer embrace the idea.

This type of "believe in a certain way or else" scenario is pointed out by Walsch as the basis of fear-based religions where God is punishing, punitive, vengeful, and jealous. Many times, I was told God loved us unconditionally, and that we should be grateful He did. However, the reality presented in the Christianity I was raised in, claimed that His love was quite conditional. If God was God, I thought, how could he be hurt? Why would he be angry? Sometimes, I thought that if the God I learned about in the Bible was a real person, he would be a jerk.

Walsch presents an interesting perspective on how religion has misread the nature of God. He offers this in the form of "Five Fallacies about God." When religious groups adhere to these fallacies, it creates crisis, violence, killing, and war.

FIVE FALLACIES ABOUT GOD[5]

First, you believe God needs something.

Second, you believe that God can fail to get what he needs.

Third, you believe that God has separated you from Him because you have not given Him what he needs.

Fourth, you believe that God still needs what He needs so badly that God now requires you, from your separated position, to give it to him.

Fifth, you believe that God will destroy you if you do not meet His requirements.

Reading through the CwG materials, I became convinced God communicates with us in many ways now, today and every day. He is not impotent as many religions proclaim, and limited to ancient texts and interpretations from only a specific and educated few. Not only that, I now saw that He communicates with us in other ways, in addition to the Bible. And that is one of the foundational messages of the CwG texts, that God is still communicating with us. In fact, God never stopped.

One other significant idea in the CwG material took me a while to fully accept. This is the idea that there is no such thing as right and wrong. At first, this sounds absurd. I thought some things have to be right, and other things must certainly be wrong. If not, then nothing would matter; the world would be in chaos. Walsch understands the impact of this idea and continues to explain the meaning as it is applied in an ultimate sense. For example, if a person lives in New York City and wants to go north to Boston, and begins their journey traveling directly west to Pennsylvania, they are not necessarily wrong; they are simply traveling in a direction that will not get them where they want to go. From a personal perspective, if a person wants to have a good marriage and rich family life, they will not go on every business trip offered or stay out late at night with friends several times a week. Going on trips and staying out late are not bad in and of themselves, but if a person wants to have a solid family life, they may want to reconsider their lifestyle. Just like a person heading to Pennsylvania might want to consider changing direction if they want to go to Boston. Neither is definitive "wrong," they simply are not acting in a way that supports what they ultimately want to do.

This way of looking at things makes much more sense to me now, but in the Christian fellowship group in college, we were taught that this type of thinking was not good. The term that this would fall under was "moral relativism." This indicated a person was viewing the world on a sliding scale of morality and not adhering to the moral laws of God and Christianity. It was a bad position to hold and meant the person either did not know God or did not believe what the Bible said about sin, weakening the need for redemption. However, even back then, I had some nagging thoughts about this perspective of morality. I wondered if the hardline approach was true. One example I thought about many times was the Fifth Commandment. "Thou shall not kill." This is a straight forward statement, but was it really true? We all believed the Bible in this proclamation. We should not kill anyone, right? No, never, was the typical answer. This was because the word "kill" most likely referred to murder, premeditated murder, perhaps. Killing in self-defense was acceptable, with varying degrees of acceptance of manslaughter depending on the seminary your pastor was from or the congregation's view. Besides, you may need to kill those who are threatening our freedom or faith in times of war. To me, that was moral relativism, spoken by those who supposedly opposed it. It never made sense to me.

As a child, I was taught that we had to "be good," "don't sin," and "do the right thing," with varying degrees of "or else" looming in the background. Even when I considered myself a Christian, there was the concern of punishment because I was still a sinner. The God I knew, while forgiving, was also severely and eternally judgmental. Considering the idea that there was no right or wrong rang true to me, allowing me to be myself without fear of repercussions. Well, at least outside the consequences of my actions, which was fine. I felt free. The sin factor was no longer in the way. This is how God could love us unconditionally.

Lesson 7 — God is still communicating.

THE NEXT COURSE— MIRACLES

The CwG material presents many alternative and insightful ways to view our world individually, as a group, and universally. Another book addressing similar issues was published a few years before the CwG books, titled *A Course in Miracles* (CM) by Helen Schucman and William Thetford. Both were Professors of Medical Psychology at Columbia University's College of Physicians and Surgeons in New York City.[1] The authors held conservative and atheistic beliefs and worked in a highly academic and prestigious setting. The content of their book was received similarly to Walsch as they described it as "a kind of rapid, inner dictation" written in shorthand notebooks. They were initially skeptical and had a difficult time accepting what was happening as the unusual process continued.

The topics covered in the CM material parallels the CwG books to a striking degree. One difference is that it is presented in the Christian setting with many references to Christ, God, and the Holy Spirit. In this way, it is much more palatable to the Christian tradition. Another difference is that the ideas are presented in a technical step-by-step format where the CwG material is a narrative format. I refer to the CwG books as an owner's manual style and the CM as a shop manual. The CM material presents a thought-by-thought analysis of how we think about God and ourselves, including exercises to help assimilate the concepts.

The CM text suggests the main problem today relates to the incorrect perception of separation between God and us. The book proposes a solution is to reject our misperceptions of the world as being apart from God in order to see the Truth. The truth is Love, and according to the authors, Love is all there is. In their view, sin is defined simply as a lack of love. According to the book, our view of the world is clouded by perceptions subject to the effects of time, change, beginnings, and endings, and based on interpretations. These interpretations come only from us, from our internal frame of reference, and are subjective, meaning that we create our world based on our ideas of it. By seeing the world as it really is, we can forgive and accept the world and create unity between us and God. In fact, the authors state that forgiveness is our only function. It is the only way we can be reunited with God and each other. While written in an academic and cerebral tone, many points are helpful. For example, some of the lessons center on ideas many can relate to such as, "I am never upset for the reason I think,"[2] or "I am upset because I see what is not there,"[3] or "I see only the past,"[4] or "My thoughts are images that I have made."[5]

What I admire almost as much as the ideas themselves in both the CwG and CM is the way the material is presented. In both books, the content is presented with an attitude of openness, offering the reader an opportunity to make their own decisions about the ideas. No threats, no punishment, just conveying ideas about life in an atmosphere of loving-kindness.

The CwG material and the CM were important for me in that they presented a comprehensive approach to not only who God is, but also who we are. This was accomplished outside of all organized religious settings.

Lesson 8 — There is no separation between God and us.

A WORD ABOUT AUTOMATIC WRITING

When I read Walsch's account of how he developed the CwG material, I was skeptical, to say the least. According to Walsch, his hand began writing on the note pad he had used to record his frustrations and questions. How did that work? I wondered about it. Did his hand just take off on its own? Could he stop it if he wanted to? The same questions come up with Helen Schucman's recounting of how the CM content was written. There are other bizarre cases too. For example, Helene Smith (real name, Catherine-Elise Muller) was a French medium living in the late 19th century who claimed she received messages from Mars in a Martian language.[1]

In my perspective, the way in which Walsch and Schucman reacted to their experiences provides enormous validity. The authors clearly conveyed how surprised they were when they started receiving and recording the material and even doubted their own authenticity. Most importantly, they offer their content as a take-it-or-leave-it manner by encouraging the reader to try it out and see what they think. This is quite the opposite of the threats of punishment or abandonment held by many of the fear-based religions and cults, insisting that their way is the Truth to be followed without exception or question. Finally, as I considered their ideas, it simply made sense and resonated with me. Also, and this is not something I share often, but much of the material in the CwG book felt familiar to me as if I was rereading it. Strange.

While not claiming to be dictated or transcribed in an automatic writing fashion, most adhering to the Evangelical-Christian tradition accept the Bible as the Word of God without question. The proof-text most often quoted is in the New Testament second book of Timothy 3:16 "All scripture is inspired by God and is useful for instruction, for conviction, for correction, and for training in righteousness." The important word here is "inspired" and referring to the original Greek language in which the text was written, the word is θεόπνευστος or theopneustos literally means "God-breathed" *theos* meaning "God," and *pneu* meaning "to breathe." This text is used as the cornerstone in many fundamentalist and Evangelical Christian churches, schools, and other organizations and often emphasizes the Bible as containing The Truth and is the literal Word of God. Many Christian organizations require potential members to sign a Statement of Faith indicating they believe the Bible to be without error, solidifying the idea that the Bible is not from the hand or mind of humans, but from a divine source. Signing a Statement of Faith is a strong reinforcement of tenacious knowing because the person signing is publicly committing themselves to a specific set of beliefs.

It is important to note that the idea of information coming from outside of a person occurs in other disciplines as well. One well-known example is Albert Einstein. Born in a Jewish family, his interests in religion expanded to his scientific beliefs. However, it was his perspective on the connection of science and divinity, where he appeared to blur the lines between humanity and something larger. For example, in these two quotes[2]:

> "There remains something subtle, intangible and inexplicable. Veneration for this force beyond anything that we can comprehend is my religion."

> "When the solution is simple, God is answering."

Another remarkable example of content coming to a person from outside themselves is in the life of Srinivasa Ramanujan in the early part of the 20th century. The story was conveyed in the book *The Man Who Knew Infinity* by Robert Kanigel and the subsequent movie released by Matt Brown in 2015.[3]

Raised in the impoverished city of Madras, India, Ramanujan was struggling to make a living in menial jobs when an employer noticed he had exceptional skills in mathematics. His employer was so impressed; he sent samples of Ramanujan's mathematical work to the renowned mathematician G.H. Hardy at England's Cambridge University in hopes Ramanujan would be recognized for his talent. The plan worked. Ramanujan moved to Cambridge, and after several years struggling with a foreign culture and lack of formal academic training, he was accepted as a Fellow of the college.

The fascinating part of this story related to the ongoing conflict Hardy and Ramanujan engaged in throughout his years at Cambridge. The disagreements centered on Ramanujan's inability to provide backup work or proofs that typically support complex mathematical formulas in academic settings. While many of the academics at Cambridge agreed that Ramanujan's work was exceptional and at a near-genius level, the lack of back-up work was causing great consternation. For a long time, Ramanujan refused to tell Hardy how he was able to produce such exceptional work, until one day he explained that he received his inspiration and understanding from a divine source. The answers came to him when he dreamed he was in the presence of the god Narasimha and "scrolls containing the most complicated mathematics would unfold before his eyes"[4] This divine goddess showed Ramanujan the formulas, and he understood them. The struggle was in showing how current mathematical theories were connected to his answers. Ramanujan conveyed an interesting thought that mimics Einstein's quote:

> "An equation for me has no meaning unless it expresses a thought of God."[5]

There are other examples of humans receiving inspiration and even direct communication from sources seemingly outside of themselves, some occurring within the Christian tradition. One is the phenomena of speaking in tongues recorded in the New Testament in the book of the Acts of the Apostles. The narrative states that approximately fifty days after Jesus came back to life and ascended into heaven, the Holy Spirit descended on the disciples in the form of tongues of fire, which appeared over each of them as they began to speak in several different languages. Other accounts in the Bible state the sounds were unintelligible. This practice occurs today in Christian Pentecostal churches, although the exact practice and format is not consistent and can be controversial.

So, what can we make of these external sources of inspiration, communication, and information? Are they from God, alien beings, or some sort of higher level of our collective consciousness? Assuming the authors were not psychotic, delusional, or high when they recorded their content, are the sources the same or different? And can we be sure the authors wrote down the thoughts without imposing any of their own biases or beliefs? It's an important point to remember — this same scrutiny can and should be applied to all the religious texts and experiences found in the world's organized religions, as well as those outside the main religions such as the texts of Neal Donald Walsch, Schucman, or Ramanujan.

The 900 followers of Jim Jones and his Peoples Temple were apparently convinced that taking the cyanide-laced punch was a good idea at the time but ended up being participants in the Jonestown Massacre of 1978. There are many other examples, spanning religious and non-religious groups lead by charismatic leaders who exploit, harm and brainwash their followers to give their time, money, and even their lives to whatever cause they are promoting.

This leaves the rest of us wondering how anyone could be duped to such an extreme degree to buy into such nonsense. However, just as this has happened in the past, it will happen in the future. But how can we determine the good from the bad? The real from the fake?

Criteria that can be used to evaluate these various sources is simple. The first is a lack of demands any organization imposes on people. Certainly, most fear-based religions contain mandates in order to be accepted by God, to avoid punishment, hell, or damnation. In light of that, the take-it-or-leave-it approach provides strong validation. People of any organization or belief system should be able to believe, doubt, come, go, or participate to whatever degree they prefer, without fear of retribution. Another way to determine if a belief system is founded on positive principals is from the New Testament book of 1 Corinthians 13:4-7. These verses are presented at many Christian weddings as the 15-point definition of love. Applying these characteristics to any belief system can provide a good idea of their intentions.

THE 15-POINT DEFINITION OF LOVE
1. Patient
2. Kind
3. Does not envy
4. Does not boast
5. Not proud
6. Does not dishonor others
7. Not self-seeking
8. Not easily angered
9. Does not delight in evil

10. Keeps no record of wrongs
11. Rejoices with the truth
12. Always protects
13. Always trusts
14. Always hopes
15. Always perseveres

Lesson 9 — Validation of any belief system can be accomplished by applying the criteria of love.

ANGEL, REALIZED

Understanding that my strivings for God originated from my psychological drives of *acceptance, curiosity, order, and tranquility*, I could see how conservative Christianity initially addressed these needs. Especially, the need for *order* because it reconciled the sin, eternal judgment, and forgiveness equation. However, after several years of trying to force-fit everyone into a rigid belief system, the same strivings that led me to Evangelical Christianity propelled me to seek answers beyond religion.

Embracing the idea that God was still communicating with us was one of two milestone insights for me. The content presented in CwG and CM rang true, and I felt comfortable about their sources being outside the Bible. I was finally free from organized religion and open to exploring other ideas about God.

The other breakthrough was accepting the idea that we are not separate from God. We are expressions of God and children of God. This means that sin is not in the equation, and therefore there is no need for salvation. There is nothing to be saved from.

"How do you know you are not going to hell?" Mom asked, during one of our discussion/interrogation sessions. Mom's typically squinty eyes peered at me.

"Because I just know. I do not believe God is judgmental, and his love is not conditional."

"What do you mean?" she shot back, as usual.

"Ok, maybe this will help. Let me ask you a question. Is there anyone on this planet who can say I am not your son?"

"Of course not," she replied.

"Is there anything that I could do that would cause you or Dad to say, I am not your son?"

"No, never. Of course not," she affirmed.

"That is the best example of my relationship with God. That is unconditional love and acceptance. I have no fear of judgment. Everything I go through in this life or after I die is all about learning and growth."

"So, you don't have to do anything? Go to church, read the Bible, pray to Jesus?" Her anxiety level was rising; her voice shaky.

"I can do these things, and I do. I enjoy doing them. I just don't *have* to do them to appease God."

Blank stare from Mom.

"Here's another example. Remember that time Glenn and I were playing, and I knocked over that vase Grandma gave you?"

"Yes, your father and I were very upset," she recalled.

"Yes, you were. You sent me to my room and no TV for a week. But suppose every week after that for months I came to you and Dad asking for forgiveness. And I would plead 'I'm clumsy, I break things, and please forgive me.'"

"We would say we forgave you, but after a few weeks, we might wonder if there was something wrong with you. We might send you a shrink." This she said with a smirk because she knew it would get to me.

"Well, the term is psychologist, but yes, something would be wrong, wouldn't it?"

"Yes, a child should have no doubts their parents love them." She said confidently.

"But at the same time, we go to church every week confessing to God we are sinners deserving punishment, and asking for forgiveness. Every week. But that is not what God is like; he is like a parent with a child. I have no doubts that you and Dad love me, and that God loves me too."

"Wow, that is really something, Scott. I don't know what to think about this," she said, looking into the distance. "I just hope you're okay."

"Yes, Mom. I'm okay. I love you."

"I love you too, boy. My youngest son," she said, as we hugged goodbye.

These insights, combined with my experiences and what I learned, were laser-focused. I realized I was truly a part of God; there was no separation. There is no sin or need for forgiveness. We are all divine beings on a journey to learn how to be more loving and less hurtful, and the journey can span hundreds of lifetimes

As Dr. Wayne Dyer, a well-known author, and speaker on spiritual growth stated,

"We are all spiritual beings living a temporary physical existence."

Lesson 10 — We are all Angels.

PRAYER 2.0— ATTRACTION

The next challenging question I began to wrestle with was; if we were angels and not separate from God, then who should we pray to get what we want to be, do, or have? I knew from reviewing hundreds of studies on prayer; the results were not as consistent as one would hope. Also, if there is no separation between God and us, whom exactly are we praying to? Was there an alternative to prayer that might fit this new paradigm? As has happened at other times in my life when struggling with a question, I would stumble onto something that helped me find the answer. This time, I stumbled on the Law of Attraction (LoA).

The LoA, also known as the power of intention, is the idea that we create all experiences in our lives by applying consistent thoughts and feelings about each aspect. For example, if we want to have a job that is positive and interesting, by consistently picturing ourselves in a position we want, eventually the opportunity will present itself. Or, if a person regularly complains about their job, telling others how bad it is, they will remain in that unpleasant situation. In its most simplistic form, the term "what goes around, comes around" captures this idea. I believe there is something worth exploring in the LoA. In this chapter, I will review the concept from several aspects from different authors.

I learned about the LoA when the book *The Secret* by Rhonda Byrne became popular after its release in 2006. It was getting some play in the press after being on the *New York Times* bestseller list for 190 weeks. What puzzled me was not the length of time on the list, but at what point in time would this no longer be a secret? I continued to be intrigued by the attention surrounding the enormously popular secret message.

In the first few pages of the book, Byrne explains that her life was in a state of ruin when her daughter gave her a book written in 1910 by a little-known author. The book was *The Science of Getting Rich* by Wallace D. Wattles. After Byrne read about the concepts presented by Wattles, she conducted extensive historical research to see if these concepts were present in any other philosophies, religions, or cultures. The results of her research proved fruitful, and she then developed the content of *The Secret*, eventually translated into over 40 languages, along with the development of several companion books.

The concepts Wattles presented are both simple and revolutionary. Similar to the CwG material, they represent a significant step away from the theological frameworks of the world's largest organized religions (Christianity, Islam, Hinduism, and Buddhism), yet according to Byrne, components from the core tenants of these religions are embedded in *The Secret's* ideas. The fundamental concept of Wattle's work revolves around the idea that we can get whatever we want through wealth, and that obtaining wealth is accomplished by"...doing things in a Certain Way."[1]

Wattles' main concepts are contained in three points repeated several times throughout his book.

> "There is a thinking stuff from which all things are made, and which, in its original state, permeates, penetrates, and fills the interspaces of the universe.
>
> A thought, in this substance, produces the thing that is imagined by the thought.
>
> Man can form things in his thought, and, by impressing his thought upon formless substance, can cause the thing he thinks about to be created."[2]

The term Law of Attraction is not contained in Wattles' work, but the concept is presented throughout. One aspect that Wattles emphasizes in his work is often left out of other LoA content; that action is critical for the process.

"By thought, the thing you want is brought to you; by action you receive it."[3]

According to Wattles, thought alone will not magically make something physically appear in front of you, but circumstances will come together serendipitously to bring you what you have been envisioning. He provides an example of a person who wants a new sewing machine. If a person holds a detailed mental image of a sewing machine, coupled with the feeling of unquestionable certainty, it will come to them. Possibly, they will meet someone that happens to have a sewing machine for sale, or some other opportunity will appear where a sewing machine will become available. So, in Wattles' perspective, thoughts bring about the opportunity, but the person still has to act to obtain what they want. In this example, the person has to take the action of connecting with the owner of the sewing machine, getting the money, and arranging to meet and completing the transaction.

Another significant source of information on the LoA comes from a different realm. Wanting to learn more, I quickly found a significant source of information in the LoA material developed by Esther and Jerry Hicks. The authors produced several books, audiotapes, videos, and conducted hundreds of workshops throughout the United States. Since the Hicks published their work in the late 80s, several years before *The Secret*, I focused on their work next.

In their book, *Ask and it Shall be Given,* the Hicks explain how they developed the content of the LoA. The process was similar to Walsch's experience in writing the CwG books, through an automatic writing process. Esther initially typed the content as the words came to her, later she would verbalize the material directly. One big difference is that while Walsch presents his source as God, Esther reported her source was a group of non-physical beings or entities. These entities were never in physical form and communicated collectively as one voice calling themselves Abraham.[4]

The Hicks generated a massive number of materials related to the LoA, addressing many aspects of the concept, far too many to discuss here. However, I will present a few of their concepts, and I encourage any seeker to learn more through their books and website, listed at the end of this book.

In their work, the Hicks expand on Wattles' concept of impressing thoughts upon formless substance, resulting in bringing thoughts to fruition. They explain that this phenomenon impacts our lives and our world, whether we are aware of it or not.

The Hick's concept of the LoA is defined as, "That which is like unto itself is drawn." The first time I learned of this idea, my thought was this was contradictory to basic magnetism. With hundreds of hours playing with magnets of all shapes and sizes when I was young, I knew that it was the opposite poles of a magnet that attracted each other and the like poles repelled. On the other hand, I could see how similar things have a tendency to be grouped together, such as how like-minded people are often attracted to each other, and we tend to notice characteristics in others that reflect our attributes.

According to the Hicks, "every thought vibrates, every thought radiates a signal, and every thought attracts a matching signal back."[5] The authors provide an example of a radio tower transmitting a signal at a specific frequency and a radio being tuned to that exact station. When the transmitter and the receiver are mismatched, nothing happens, but when they are in alignment, the music flows. So it is with our thoughts, whatever we give our attention to, emits a vibration that attracts the object of our thoughts.

According to the authors, the quickest way to experience what you want is to hold consistent positive thoughts to attract it into your life, to imagine having it, and pretend it's already yours, and you are enjoying the experience. Practicing these thoughts also helps to provide a consistent vibrational offering of attraction.

This is almost identical to Wattles's idea that holding a detailed image in mind with certainty will provide what the person is envisioning. Hicks also emphasizes the LoA is in effect at all times whether a person is consciously focusing on something or not. This means that if a person is consistently ruminating about their *old broken down car*, then they will continue to experience their *old broken down car*, or if a person keeps dreaming about their wedding day having perfect weather, then they will experience ideal weather.

HOW THE LAW OF ATTRACTION WORKS

In the numerous materials presented by the Hicks, many descriptions, explanations, exercises, and tools are provided that illustrate how the concept of LoA works and how to apply it in real-life situations. Interestingly, I also discovered three ways why the LoA may not appear to work.

One reason why the LoA may not work is by a lack of clear and consistent thoughts. Many times, people get distracted and stop thinking about a particular thing or lose interest. Another way the LoA would not appear to work is because even if clear and consistent thoughts are maintained, thoughts of uncertainty and doubt will cancel out the overall vibration of the specific desire. A third reason, which was most interesting to me, is that many times people are not aware that what they are focusing on, vibrating, and manifesting about is, in fact, the opposite thing they want to experience in their lives.

For example, if a person consistently is thinking, "I want more money," or "I want to have a better job," the vibration that will manifest is the "I want" part. So, as long as the person concentrates on *wanting* to have money or a better job, that feeling of *wanting* will continue, and nothing will change. You can see why picturing yourself as *having* the thing or situation you want, and practicing these thoughts is so critical.

The Hicks state an important component of how the LoA works relates to emotions. The authors present the idea that our emotions are a sixth sense just as taste, touch, smell, sight, and hearing are senses. The main difference is that the five physical senses relate to our physical experience and emotions relate to who you are at your deepest levels, your *source*. The first step is to become aware of your emotions and specific feelings, and the second is to gain the ability to change your emotions to align more with what you want to do, be, or have.

To present their concepts, the authors provide examples of how we can improve our point of attraction, meaning how to best think and control our feelings to attract what we want in our lives. In *Ask and it is Given*, the authors provide 22 examples to help a person improve their "point of attraction." The examples outline ways to both visualize what we want, as well as show how we can monitor and change our feelings to align with our vision.

They begin by introducing the idea of assessing our emotional "set point," which is to identify how we are feeling at the moment precisely. The authors provide a sample range of 22 emotional descriptions with the highest most positive emotions, to the lowest.[1]

A SCALE OF EMOTIONS

1. Joy/Knowledge/Empowerment/Freedom/Love/Appreciation
2. Passion
3. Enthusiasm/Eagerness/Happiness
4. Positive Expectations/Belief
5. Optimism
6. Hopefulness
7. Contentment
8. Boredom
9. Pessimism
10. Frustration/Irritation/Impatience
11. "Overwhelment"
12. Disappointment
13. Doubt
14. Worry
15. Blame
16. Discouragement
17. Anger
18. Revenge
19. Hatred/Rage
20. Jealousy
21. Insecurity
22. Fear/Greif/Depression/Despair/Powerlessness

By identifying our starting emotional status as a baseline, we can not only choose the best example that matches our emotional level at the time, but we can assess how effective the exercises are in elevating our emotional status. For example, the exercise titled "Finding the Feeling Place" is designed for people who want to improve their situation to receive more money, a better job, happier relationship, or better-feeling body. This exercise is meant for people who have an emotional baseline or set point on the low end of the scale of between #9 Pessimism to #17 Anger. The goal of this exercise is to create images of the times when you had what you now want or to envision yourself having them. In other words, spend time in the *feeling place* that you want. The authors mention taking small steps, not leaps to increase emotional levels gradually. By doing this, your emotional set point will improve.

Interestingly, The Universe, according to the authors, does not discern whether the vibrations offered are from an actual life situation or if it is imagined. In either case, it will provide according to the vibrations offered. The idea of projecting oneself into a desired experience is also depicted in the familiar term "fake it until you make it," found in other self-help programs.

The authors' explanation of coupling a precise and consistent vision of what we want with equally consistent feelings, is like a sculptor who learns to mold clay into the piece they want to create. According to the authors, this is how we shape our lives out of the people we meet, and the events and opportunities we experience.

The Hicks state we are the creators of our experiences, without exception. This leads to many questions that explain unwanted events in our lives like death, disease, accidents, loss of jobs, or lifetimes spent on unsuccessful pursuits. None of the LoA authors provide a clear answer to the question of why a person would be consciously or unconsciously sending out vibrations of harm, disease, or horrific events.

"You're telling me that I *asked* for all this?" Trisha said, so upset her voice shot up in volume and was shaking, her eyes started to tear up. Her response stunned me because it came on so suddenly and with great emotion. Trisha and Jeremy lived next door along with their three young children. My wife and I spent many afternoons and evenings with them for many years. We would share every detail of our lives, talking about jobs, kids, politics, and life.

That particular night, I was talking about a new concept I was learning about, the LoA. I went into great detail about how it came to be, who Esther and Jerry Hicks were, as well as Abraham, and how it all was supposed to work. Trisha and Jeremy were listening and asking questions, as usual, providing their perspectives and digging deeper into the concept. At one point in the conversation, I was explaining how the authors clearly stated all experiences that appear in our lives come to us through our emotional offerings to the Universe, without exception. In my description, I confidently applied the LoA concepts and spoke about finding the right car, job or spouse. That is when Trisha exploded. A split second later, we all knew exactly why she reacted so strongly, and why it derailed that part of the discussion. A family member had emotionally and sexually abused Trisha for many years when she was a child. The trauma, as anyone would expect, had a devastating impact on her throughout her life.

"Ah, I don't . . . I don't know what to say, Trisha. I'm sorry. I don't know what to say, I don't have any answers." Offering my lame reply, still reeling from the exchange.

"It's ok, Scott. No one can explain it; no one knows why." I think she saw my dismay, and let me off the hook.

My guess is, if pressed on this situation, the authors of the LoA would answer by saying that everyone is on their own journey, and we cannot know why things happen to others or what reason or purpose unwanted events may hold. To be fair, no religion has a clear answer on how an omnipotent and loving God allows terrible things like what Trisha experienced to occur.

After gaining a good understanding of the LoA from the Hicks, I turned my attention back to Byrne's work contained in *The Secret*. Byrne states the secret is, in fact, the LoA, and describes similar core principles as in the Hicks' model. One significant contribution she offers traces the LoA concept through history. She provides examples of how it was used by the world's greatest minds like Plato, Shakespeare, Newton, Lincoln, and Einstein, among others.[2] A compelling component of her work is how she offers several quotes and content from over 20 thought leaders in philosophy, physics, and literature, all providing further explanations and validation of the LoA concept.

Byrne also explains the LoA is a law of nature and is in effect at all times whether a person is aware of it or not, just as the Hicks present. She uses the same Hicks analogy of the radio tower, stating we are continually sending powerful signals of our thoughts out to the universe, and the content of our thoughts is subsequently manifested in our lives. Byrne also agrees with the Hicks in the idea of people not getting what they want because they focus their thoughts more on what they don't want than what they do want. Similar to the example of a person fixated on *wanting* to be, do, or have something, will perpetuate the *wanting* experience rather than the experience of *having*.

According to Byrne, the same concept works if thoughts are focused on *not wanting* something. This is because the Universe does not recognize negative words like don't, not, or no. For example, if a person places their attention on *not wanting an unreliable car,* the Universe responds to the thought of *wanting* an unreliable car, leaving the *not* out, and will continue to provide the experience of an unreliable car.

I noticed an interesting correlation with this idea to something I learned when I was training to become a hypnotherapist. The theory was that the unconscious mind does not recognize negatives and perceives things as absolute values. An excellent example of how this translated to therapy was when a person needed help to stop smoking. We were taught to not focus on *stopping* smoking but to guide the client's visualizations to see themselves as a healthy and fit person. All references to stopping smoking, quitting smoking, or no longer smoking would be reinforcing *smoking*.

While emotions are critical in Byrne's process as they are in Hicks, she does not give as much attention to specific terminology to convey the various emotions. The most important emotions for Byrne are gratitude and thankfulness. As she states, "Gratitude is a powerful process for shifting your energy and bringing more of what you want into your life."[3] Also, she says that when you strongly feel as though you have what you are looking for, as if you already have it, you are believing that you have it and will, therefore, receive the object of your attention.

As with any theory, there are supporters and critics. One critic of the LoA is Neal Farber MD, Ph.D., a highly prolific writer on positive psychology, as well as a researcher on topics related to creating a positive work environment, mindfulness, goal-setting, productive communication, and positive parenting. In a 2014 article in *Psychology Today*, Farber provides an oversimplified and sarcastic review of the concept of the LoA and states that the success rate for those using the LoA is small, citing a statistic of 0.1% success rate.[4] He does not provide any references for this percentage.

In the article, Farber goes on to promote his theory, the "Principle of Attraction." His principle is a watered-down version of the LoA, stating that "like tends to attract like, positivity usually attracts positivity," and "negativity usually attracts negativity," centering around the idea of positive thinking.

It appears that Farber adhered to his principle of "negativity usually attracts negativity" by publishing a follow-up article in September of 2016 in *Psychology Today* titled, "The Truth About the Law of Attraction."[5] In this article, he continues his obvious bias against LoA, listing 14 reasons why the LoA does not exist. Farber's descriptions of the reasons are overwhelmingly critical and sarcastic to the point where, unfortunately, in my opinion, his credibility as a valid voice in the discussion is not useful. He ends his article, as with the first, with the unreferenced statistic of 0.1% success rate for the LoA, along with a plug for his newest book.

Dr. Wayne Dyer developed several books on the topic of the LoA. However, Dr. Dyer uses the term "Power of Intention" and offers a slightly different and broader perspective on this practice. The biggest mistake people make in approaching the LoA, according to Dr. Dyer, is they want and demand things. He goes on to state, "The law of attraction is this: You don't attract what you want. You attract what you are."[6]

In the Power of Intention material, Dr. Dyer states that in order to realize our desires, we must first align our thoughts and feelings with our inner selves. Then, we act as if we already have what we desire. In this perspective, it is all about *allowing*, not *demanding*. Our action is more passive than directive, cultivated in an attitude of reverence for all life, sincerity, gentleness, and supportiveness.

In terms of the four ways we can obtain knowledge about the LoA, there are many anecdotes and stories from people detailing how the LoA impacted their lives (authority). Also, many will hold fast to the idea that the LoA works or doesn't work (tenacity), and still others will have an innate understanding or acceptance of the idea (a priori). There will remain others who will want to see evidence and proof of the concept before accepting it as a viable theory (scientific observation).

THREE EXPERIMENTS WITH LOA

I was intrigued by the material offered on the topic of LoA, in terms of both the definitions and the many methods proposed in order to help people align their vibrations to obtain the things they wanted. So, I decided to do some experiments on my own, with some interesting results. My sample size was one, and I was the lead investigator and participant. This does not fall into the category of good research design, but it was something.

I was working for a company that developed a medication adherence program to help people commit to taking their medications. Organizations that pay for the care of people, such as insurance companies, health systems, or employers, are interested in programs that will help keep their patients adherent to their medication schedule, and therefore healthy. However, any company that offered a program similar to ours faced a catch-22 situation. This is when the potential buyer might want to implement a program but wanted to see results from previous studies before committing. As a result, we needed a contract with someone willing to pay for a program with no evidence to support its success. That was my intention, my desire: a contract with one group or company to pilot our program.

Following the directions from the LoA materials, I took time each day to quiet my mind and visualize having a contract with an organization for our program. Many times with meditative music playing in the background, I pictured a call coming through from one of our contacts who were excited to pilot the program, and I spent many hours visualizing precisely how we would introduce the program to the company's medical staff, human resource staff, and middle managers. I pictured myself and the situations completely, not only imagining the sights and sounds but the smells and textures of the rooms where I would make these presentations. Some days I wasn't able to have a quiet moment, but overall, I was able to devote 10-15 mins a day for at least five days per week on the visualization process.

Weeks and months passed with us making presentations to dozens of companies and organizations. We always got the same response. "Come back when you have some data that shows this works." About six months after I began my regular visualization rituals, it happened. We were notified that a health system in Connecticut was willing to pilot the program with its 3,000 employees. If the program produced positive results after six months, they would open it up to other groups. This was our break. We were confident that if even one component of the program worked, which there were about a dozen, it would be considered a success and rolled out within a year or two to hundreds of thousands of people covered by the health system. I was ecstatic. It was an incredible project and opportunity, and we were all excited as we began to execute implementation plans and meetings to roll out the program.

This could be viewed as evidence the LoA worked. But maybe it was just our hard work that "manifested" the opportunity. Perhaps this was just a coincidence that randomly occurred by chance from the dozens of presentations we made. The fanatical supporters of LoA would make a big deal about these occurrences, claiming they were the results of the vibrations I offered. It was tough to tell and impossible to know for sure. But then something else happened.

About two weeks after we got the notification for the pilot, we were meeting with another health system. They informed us that they too wanted to pilot the program with their employees. They cited the same offer, to expand to their hundreds of thousands of customers if the initial results were positive. With the odds against us landing any contracts with our untested program, now the second contract appeared on my desk. I couldn't help but wonder if this was further evidence of LoA. It still could have been the result of our efforts. But the results of random chance? Less likely. I concluded it might not be concrete proof, but definitely was worth further consideration.

The second experiment I conducted was much shorter. My desire, this time, was winning the Powerball lottery. I applied the same process used in the medication adherence contracts as the lottery approached $400 million. For 10-15 min a day, with meditation music in the background, I visualized the things I would do if I won all that money in as much detail as possible. It all ended after about two weeks when someone in the Midwest won the money. I have no idea why it didn't work. Although I have always had doubts about how well I would handle being a multimillionaire.

The third experiment I conducted involved one of the loves of my life, motorcycles. And I applied the same meditation program for this experiment I used for in my other two, but this time it lasted ten months.

The study began in June of 2015 when I was at a motorcycle rally with some friends in Lake George, New York. It was a typical rally with thousands of motorcycle enthusiasts attending and participating in special events, several motorcycle manufacturers were there as well, offering their latest models.

The bike I had then was a 15-year-old Honda Gold Wing, and even though I knew I couldn't afford it, I was interested in the new model. Gold Wings are large, expensive touring bikes specifically made for long rides. I went to the

Honda booth to schedule a test drive of the new model the next morning.

As any motorcycle enthusiast has experienced, this ride was as close to love at first sight as one can get. I loved the power on the highway and the way it glided smoothly on the back roads. I was hooked. When I got back to the booth, I learned this was a new model, the F6B and cost around $20,000. I had no idea how I would pay for it, but I committed to myself that I would come back to the same rally the next year riding my new bike.

I quickly began the process of attraction I used for my other experiments. It was easy to visualize what I wanted because I experienced it on the test drive. The big question was how to pay for it. Maybe my annual bonus, I thought, but in the past, it had never been large enough to cover the cost of a new Gold Wing. When I had those thoughts, I reminded myself that doubts could short-circuit the positive vibrations of attraction. Otherwise, I would have been a millionaire by now by winning the lottery.

Months later, the riding season ended, and winter set in. I was regularly working on my desire with certainty, overriding my doubts, and believing that I would be riding my new bike in the spring. That December, I found a dealer near me that had it, and I asked about the price. My dream bike was going to cost me $22,000. Nevertheless, battling this new round of doubts that could ruin my vision, I told the sales guy I would be in to see it soon. December was also when we scheduled our year-end reviews at work. A year-end bonus would go a long way to help fund my dream because it was the only way I could get the cash infusion I needed.

ANGEL IN TRAINING

I had my review, and it went well. My manager told me that the bonuses would be good since we had an exceptional year. She would let me know in the middle of March what the number would be. This was it. The stage was set. Spring was around the corner, the bike I wanted was sitting in a showroom about 10 miles from my home, and a bonus was coming my way. I even booked the trip to the same rally where I first rode the same model the year before, and where I vowed to return this year on my new wheels.

When it came time for my manager to call me into her office to tell me about my bonus, I was dumbfounded. Unbelievable. The bonuses that year were higher than any other year in the company's history. The bonus I received was $22,000. It was the exact price of my dream bike—$22,000.

Does this prove the LoA? No. As any scientifically minded person will say, we can't prove anything. We can say this experiment supports the concept of the LoA mainly because several variables had to align for my vision to become a reality. I had no idea and no control over what my bonus would be. The fact that it matched the cost of my bike was remarkable.

Several weeks after I got the bike, my manager was walking by as I was parking my new two-wheeler at work. On the walk into the office, I briefly explained the concept of LoA and my experiment. Being an opened minded person, she seemed to at least not rule the idea out. I went further and asked if she happened to know somehow that I was looking for a new bike and got me the money I needed. She told me I was an idiot to think that she found out the type of bike I was looking for, do the research, select a model, get an average price, and put in for that amount. Okay, I got it. It had been a ridiculous thing to ask her. But I had to ask.

In thinking about the LoA and whether it is a real and consistent phenomenon, it occurred to me this could be an alternative to what prayer is supposed to do. In this case, the focus is not a deity; the focus is becoming aware of our thoughts and emotions to create the outcomes we want. In the spirit of research, I emailed the Abraham-Hicks organization to ask if they would be interested in conducting a study to validate the LoA concepts. The organization replied that they do not get involved in any research relating to the LoA. They did not provide any other explanation or comment. The more I thought about it; I realized it would be harder to study the effects of LoA than prayer because of the subjectivity of the variables. Developing a set of questions that would quantify a person's emotional state that matched the LoA's 22 emotional descriptions, and detect changes, would be challenging to validate.

LOA TAKEAWAYS

For me, the first takeaway is the LoA and intention are concepts worth spending time experimenting with and exploring. One reason for this is its simplicity. The fourteenth-century philosopher William Ockham proposed the idea that when considering several solutions to complicated issues, the simplest solution will be the most successful. This theory is called Ockham's Razor, or the Law of Parsimony and is used in developing scientific theory. The simplicity of the LoA is that it states that what you project, you will receive. The statement "what goes around comes around" follows this idea, and I believe many of us have seen this play out in our lives and the lives of others.

A second takeaway is that the LoA provides an explanation of why there are 4,500 different religions around the world. These diverse belief systems work because their followers hold clear and consistent thoughts about expectations of their particular religion, experience something positive, and are committed to their faith. Whatever the person believes in, if their thoughts align with their beliefs and emotions, the LoA will provide.

A third takeaway is that the LoA could explain why many prayer studies don't work. If a person prays to be cured of an infection, the vibration will resonate with *infection* and so it will persist. As in the large STEP bypass surgery prayer study, the people who were prayed for to have "no complications" had the most complications of the three study groups because the dominant vibration was *complications*.

A fourth takeaway is that the LoA could explain how hurtful and angry people are successful. The reason is they are aligned with their thoughts, energy, and emotions to create the experiences they want, even though it is not desirable from other people's perspectives.

An important note to remember is that the authors of the LoA and intention point out that these concepts are in place even if we are not consciously focused on them. Just as a sailboat will meander through the water if no one is controlling the rudder or sail, many people go through life the same way.

Getting back to the fundamental question, can we manifest things just by thinking about them? The answer is clear, it depends. What we are thinking about, what we want to see in our lives, how long have we been focused and with what level of intensity, in addition to any underlying doubts, all come into play.

In any case, the concept of LoA, at least theoretically and intuitively make sense enough for me to consider and continue to experiment within different scenarios. At the bare minimum, it encourages us to hold a positive attitude as we seek to be, do, or have things we would like to experience.

Lesson 11 — The Law of Attraction and power of intention are simple concepts with universal applications.

A QUANTUM EXPLANATION

One consistent question in my spiritual journey was; to what degree we can influence, control, or manipulate our world? I saw the evidence of how prayer and meditation could impact physical and mental conditions, but what about life situations the LoA claims to be able to accomplish? This is the difference between praying for good health and seeing health conditions improve, compared to wanting a specific car and then bumping into someone at the store, and learning that one of their neighbors was moving and was selling the exact make and model.

From a religious perspective, the underlying mechanism of action in prayer is divine intervention. However, in the LoA, it is the Universe and the movement of energy that affects change. Assuming this is accurate, the next questions relate to, how does this work? And are there any guiding principles to help explain these phenomena? After some searching, I was surprised to learn there is a discipline that provides some light on these questions, as well as possible answers. This is the study of quantum physics, also known as quantum mechanics, or quantum theory.

The reason quantum physics is central in this exploration is that it provides a possible explanation of how our thoughts, prayers, and meditations might impact our world. Importantly, it reveals how the act of observing can change the world we see.

Before we delve into this topic, it's helpful to look at how we got to quantum physics from "regular" physics. As we all know from grade school, the study of physics started with Isaac Newton when he presented his laws of motion in 1896. Stemming from the supposed apple falling on his head; Newton's work is identified as *classical physics* and centers on the movement of objects. His theories helped organize and predict the position and speed of objects in any timeframe in addition to accounting for the impact of gravity. From this perspective, the world is viewed as a series of mechanical objects with all movements and motions able to be predicted and manipulated. This thinking ignited the Scientific Revolution of the 1600s and the subsequent Industrial Revolution, which transformed the world through advances in the development of machinery, equipment, and productivity.

However, when scientists started looking more closely at how objects worked at the subatomic level, specifically at the behavior of atoms and their components, they found the physical world at this level did not operate exactly as Newton suggested in his classical theories.

Three findings challenged Newtonian theories at the subatomic levels and ushered in the discipline of quantum mechanics. One observation relates to the basic physical principle that when an object is heated, it emits light. The more heat applied, the more light is released. In studying this effect, the German physicist, Max Planck, was the first to discover that light was not emitted in smooth and continuously increasing energy waves when an object was heated. Albert Einstein confirmed this idea with his work on the Photoelectric Effect, showing that light is not a continual wave, but clumps of energy he called "photons." These acted as particles as they traveled through space.

Another example that contradicted classical physics is in work by Danish physicist Niels Bohr, in his studies of the hydrogen atom. This atom is simple because it has one electron orbiting around one proton. Bohr noted that, according to classical physics, the atom should be continually emitting radiation or light as the electron loses energy and collapses into the proton, but this was not how the electron behaved. What was happening was the electron emitted more or less energy depending on the size of its orbits and emitted no energy if it was in a stable orbit, opposite of what classical physics predicted.

Not too long after these discoveries were made, another aspect of light was revealed that shook the traditional ideas of physics to an even greater extent. The finding was made in the famous double-slit experiment, first conducted by Davisson and Germer in 1927. In this experiment, a beam of electrons was shown through a board containing two vertical slits and projected on a screen. The classical physics model predicted the light on the screen would be concentrated directly opposite each of the slits, showing just two lines of light on the screen. However, what appeared was a series of several bright and dark bands. The explanation for this was the light coming through the slits did not move in a straight line as particles, but changed to behave as waves that either joined or canceled waves from the neighboring slit. This produced several bands of light on the screen, just like two intersecting ripples in a pond. The results of these experiments, in addition to Einstein's Photoelectric Effect and Plank's work in blackbody radiation, revealed that light could act as a wave and a particle depending on the environment.

Even more interesting was what happened when scientists attempted to observe precisely when the shift from particle to wave occurred as the electrons passed through the slits. As mentioned, when the stream of electrons passed through the slits, they changed from particles to waves. But when exactly did this change happen? To answer this question, scientists set up observation points before, after, and at the slits to see when the shift occurred. The results showed that at whatever point the electrons were observed, they would act as particles. When they weren't observed while passing through the slits, they would transition to waves. This means that even after the electrons passed through the slits and were acting like waves, once observation began, they would revert to particle behavior. In scientific terms, the act of observation caused the collapse of the wave function. These discoveries led German physicist Werner Heisenberg to present the principle called the Observation Effect, suggesting we can change the behavior of physical systems through observation.

Quantum theory takes us to a different place when considering how we interact with the world around us. There are four areas from the quantum shift where we can glean valuable insights.

OUR PERCEPTION OF OUR WORLD IS INCOMPLETE

Drs. Deepak Chopra and Menas Kafatos, in their book *You are the Universe*,[1] propose that our brains are limited in their ability to record all aspects of our surroundings. For example, visible light represents only .01 percent of the electromagnetic spectrum. This means that our eyes are not able to see the bulk of all the frequencies that engulf us in the form of gamma rays, radio waves, x-rays, and microwaves. The authors also point out that there is no light inside our skulls. Our cranium only contains our brain, which assembles signals from our eyes and optical network to create the experience of light. Our brains organize information from all sensory inputs (sight, taste, touch, hearing, and smell) to create our experiences. This means we are always one step removed from reality. Just as a picture or video of an ocean is not the ocean, but an image processed through camera sensors, our perception is not reality, but a combination of sensory inputs used to create the reality.

WE CHANGE THINGS BY OBSERVING THEM

While the Observation Effect in physics showed how the behavior of light is impacted by observation, applications can be seen in other disciplines as well. An example comes from social psychology with the Hawthorne Effect. Henry Landsberger developed the term in 1958 as he reviewed the results of productivity studies at the Hawthorne

Works factory owned by General Electric near Chicago, Illinois.[2] The factory management wanted to explore ways to improve productivity, and they started by observing lighting conditions. Their studies showed that workers increased productivity as the brightness of light in the room increased. Wanting to learn more, they conducted additional studies and found that productivity also increased when changes in workstations were made, and break times were adjusted. Landsberger made two other observations that caused him to question the impact of the workplace changes on their ultimate productivity. One was that productivity decreased after the study concluded, and second, sometimes productivity increased even when the workplace changes reverted to the original setting. He concluded that the workers worked harder because they knew they were being observed. In other words, by simply observing the workers, their productivity changed.

WE ARE INTERCONNECTED WITH THE WORLD WE PERCEIVE

Nobel Prize laureate and physicist Niels Bohr expands on the concept of the impact of observation, stating that we can never have total knowledge of the world because as we observe something, we change the thing we are observing. According to Bohr, quantum physics can only make predictions and observations, but cannot explain anything about the world we assume to exist outside of our observations.

Bohr provides a startling insight stating that any event we experience and observe must be seen as an interconnected totality. Meaning that the observer and the object are interacting with each other.[3] Einstein's theories support this idea by showing that matter is another form of energy. This suggests that reality is an interaction of physical material and energy.[4] In other words, as stated by Drs. Chopra and Kafatos, "We project ourselves into everything we experience, not just by observing, but by participating in the reality that emerges."[5]

WE DON'T KNOW WHAT WE DON'T KNOW

Some people question the ideas of the LoA, observation effect, and an interconnected reality, saying they are unscientific. While it's always good to apply some level of skepticism to new ideas, we must remember that science is only our latest best guess of how our world works. We learn about significant discoveries every year that take us far beyond anyone thought possible. In reality, we have a long way to go to understand many things; some relate to the most fundamental components of our world. As Dr. Caleb Scharf, director of astrobiology at Columbia University[6], points out, we don't know what dark energy is, and it comprises over 68% of our universe. Also, we are just starting to understand the quantum nature of reality, black holes, multiverses, and quantum firewalls. Other areas where we lack understanding is the composition and movements of material deep within the Earth's core or why we can't live without microbial cells our bodies. We do not even know completely how photosynthesis works or how it has provided life-giving oxygen to our planet for millennium. The list goes on and on. The point here is that just because we do not understand a new concept or theory, it doesn't mean it does not exist. Many times, science follows the pursuit of real phenomena.

QUANTUM TAKEAWAY

Quantum physics is a complicated topic, and an in-depth discussion is certainly beyond the scope of this book. Nevertheless, the basic principles described here suggest that reality, from our point of view, could be shifting right before our eyes. Reality is very much a subjective experience. Also, I suggest that the LoA could be the mechanism of how matter and energy interact to create the world we experience. In other words, these quantum insights propose that, as we move through our lives, what we see and experience is a fraction of what is really happening around us, and, may be changing as we go, influenced by our emotions, thoughts, and intentions.

To what extent we can change our world and how fast are the critical questions. Does this mean that if I want a used Boeing 747, one will land in my backyard? Ridiculous. However, if I'm looking for specific things or situations, and hold consistent thoughts about them, possibly, forces that we do not know about now, will align the opportunities, connections, and coincidences to bring that experience into our lives.

If so, this is a true paradigm shift in how we view ourselves in relation to the world around us and speaks to the heart of what I would like to convey in these pages.

All the lessons I have learned culminate in this final insight.

Lesson 12 — "We are co-creators of our reality because we see things not as they are, but as we are." Anaïs Nin

ON BEING ANGELS

It took about ten years for me to get this book together and on paper. I'm now in my 60s and can see the many lessons I have learned along the way and, hopefully, have conveyed them clearly. As I mentioned at the beginning of this book, I will say again, if you are satisfied with your current beliefs, religion, or practices, *please* do not make any changes. As discussed earlier, there is no right or wrong, good or bad. It's all about what you want and your happiness. Please keep in mind also, the practice of meditation, the LoA, and intention can be applied in everyone's lives independent of, and along with, any religious beliefs or traditions. Just because organized religion did not work for me, doesn't mean it can't work at all.

The most profound change I experienced as a result of my journey was the shift in perception of seeing myself as part of God, a messenger, an angel. I finally understood that God was not "out there" somewhere. I was unconditionally accepted, with no fear of judgment. The immense freedom in moving away from my fear-based religious background altered my life forever. I was enlightened.

This is not a slightly different view of God, but a huge departure from many of the belief systems that have been embedded in human culture for centuries. Paradigm shifts like this take time to become widely accepted because challenges to long-standing concepts are typically met with resistance. As stated by the famed Irish playwright, George Bernard Shaw, "All major changes in thought begin as blasphemy."

Being an angel means we fully grasp the idea we are a part of God. This is not a new idea and is embedded in several of the world's religions. Several references to our oneness with God can be found throughout the Bible. For example, in the book of John, chapter 17 verse 11, Jesus is praying before he was arrested and asked God to "... protect them by the power of your name – the name you gave me – so that they may be one as we are one."

Dr. Wayne Dwyer expands on this idea by developing a list of phrases indicative of how various religions have conveyed the concept of unity and an intimate connectedness with the "source."

> Christian—The Kingdom of God is within you.
>
> Islam—To know yourself is to know God.
>
> Buddhism—Look within, you are the Buddha.
>
> Hindu—By understanding yourself, all the universe is known.[1]

Our place in this, as described by Dr. Dyer, is that we are spiritual beings living a temporary physical existence.

ANGEL IN TRAINING

Meaning we transition between physical and spiritual lives to learn and to help others. Neal Donald Walsh also proposes that we are on an evolutionary path through many lives to learn how to exemplify positive virtues.

Being an angel means that maybe, at some point along our journey, we will be able to intervene in someone's life like the Buddhist woman did with me to convey an important message. Or, perhaps we could be in the position to cause a door to burst open, knocking someone to the floor, thwarting a devastating plan, just as happened to me.

In any case, whether you believe we live one life or many, we are all on a journey. And whether you believe our lives are following a plan, or are random events, we all have opportunities to learn, grow, and help others along the way. This is why I believe we are all . . . Angels in Training.

SCOTT GUERIN

12 LESSONS

LESSON 1:
We create our perceptions about God 167

LESSON 2:
Religion and spirituality are two distinct concepts. A person can be religious without being spiritual and spiritual without being religious. 173

LESSON 3:
There are many ways to God 184

LESSON 4:
When we understand our conflicting feelings, we can free ourselves to change 189

LESSON 5:
It is important to understand how you have decided what you believe is true 195

LESSON 6:
Meditation is a powerful and effective way to experience peace and the presence of God. It is universal, transcending all bounds of religion, theology, and belief systems. 211

LESSON 7:
God is still communicating. 225

LESSON 8:
There is no separation between
God and us 228

LESSON 9:
Validation of any belief system can
be accomplished by applying the
criteria of love. 235

LESSON 10:
We are all Angels 238

LESSON 11:
The Law of Attraction and power of
intention are simple concepts with
universal applications. 261

LESSON 12:
"We are co-creators of our reality
because we see things not as they
are, but as we are." Anaïs Nin 269

SUGGESTED READINGS

Arntz, William, Hoffman, Matthew, Chasse, Betty, and Vincente, Mark. (2004) *What the Bleep do we Know?* Captured Light and Lord of the Winds Films, LLC, 2004.

Byrne, Rhonda. *The Secret*. Atria Books/Beyond Words. 2006.

Campbell, Joseph, and Moyers, William. *Joseph Campbell and the Power of Myth with Bill Moyers*. Audio CD. Maryland: Highbridge Company, 2001.

Chopra, Deepak, and Kafatos, Menas. *You are the Universe*. New York: Harmony Books. 2017.

Dyer, Wayne. *Wisdom of the ages*. Boston: Harper Collins, 2002.

Hahn, Thich Nhat. *Living Buddha, Living Christ*. New York: Riverhead Books, 1995.

Newton, Michael. *Journey of Souls*. St. Paul, Minnesota: Llewellyn Publications, 1988.

Stevenson, Ian. *20 Cases in Support of Reincarnation (2nd ed)*. Charlottesville, VA: University Press of Virginia, 1974

Kanigel, Robert. *The man who knew infinity: a life of the genius, Ramanujan*. New York: C. Scribner's, 1991.

Hicks, Esther, and Hicks, Jerry. *Ask, and it is Given*. Carlsbad, California, Hay House, Inc. 2004.

Myss, Caroline. *Anatomy of the Spirit*. New York: Harmony Books, 1996.

Reiss, Steven. *The 16 Strivings for God*. Macon Georgia: Mercer University Press, 2015.

Thetford, William T, and Schucman, Helen. *A Course in Miracles*. Mill Valley, CA: Foundation of Inner Peace, 1975.

Walsch, Neale Donald. The Conversations with God Series

Wattles, Wallace D. *The Science of Getting Rich*. Langhorn, Pennsylvania, JonRose Publishing, 1910

Weiss, Brian. *Many Lives, Many Masters*. New York: Simon & Schuster, 1988.

REFERENCES

LOOKING INTO THE ABYSS

1. Lukoff, David, Turner, Robert, and Lu, Francis. "Transpersonal Psychology Research Review: Psychoreligious Dimensions of Healing." *The Journal of Transpersonal Psychology* 24, no.1 (1992): 41-60.

COMMONLY CONFUSED TOPICS

1. Sandra Schneiders, "Spirituality in the Academy," Theological Studies 50 (1989): 684.

2. Decker, Larry. "The Role of Trauma in Spiritual Development." *Journal of Humanistic Psychology*, 33 no. 4 (1993): 33-46.

3. Meraviglia, Martha, G. "Critical Analysis of Spirituality and its Empirical Indicators." *Journal of Holistic Nursing*, 17 no.1 (March 1999): 18-34.

What, Wait...There are others?

1. Hahn, Thich Nhat. *Living Buddha, Living Christ*. New York: Riverhead Books, 1995.

2. Stevenson, Ian. *20 Cases in Support of Reincarnation (2nd ed)*. Charlottesville, VA: University Press of Virginia, 1974

3. Weiss, Brian. *Many Lives, Many Masters*. New York: Simon & Schuster, 1988.

4. Newton, Michael. *Journey of Souls*. St. Paul, Minnesota: Llewellyn Publications, 1988.

5. Reiss, Steven. *The16 Strivings for God*. Macon Georgia: Mercer University Press, 2015.

CONTRARY TO YOUR OWN BELIEFS

1. Baron, Robert and Byrne, Dean. *Social Psychology (8th ed.)* Needham Heights: Allyn & Bacon, 1997.

HOW DO WE KNOW ANYTHING?

1. Pierce, Charles S. (1887). "The Fixation of Belief." *Popular Science Monthly*, 12, (November 1887): 1-15. http://www.peirce.org/writings/p107.html

PRAYER—THE SEQUEL

1. Keefe, Frances J., Crisson, James, Urban, Bruno J., and Williams, David A. "Analyzing chronic low back pain: The relative contribution of pain coping strategies." *Pain*, 40 no.3 (March 1990): 203-301.

2. Byrd, Randolph. "Positive therapeutic effects of intercessory prayer in a coronary care unit population." *Southern Medical Journal*, 81 no. 7 (July 1988): 826-829.

3. Carroll, S. "Spirituality and purpose in life in alcoholism recovery." *Journal of Studies on Alcohol*, 54 no. 3 (1993): 297-301.

4. Levin, JS, Lyons, JS., and Larson, DB. "Prayer and health during pregnancy: Findings from the Galveston Low Birthweight Survey." *Southern Medical Journal*, 86 no.9 (1993): 1022-1027.

5. Collipp, PJ. "The efficacy of prayer: A triple-blind study." *Medical Times*, 97 no. 5 (1969): 201-204.

6. Old Testament book of 2nd Samuel Chapter 12 verses 16-23

7. McCullough, M. (1995) "Prayer and Health: Conceptual issues, research review, and research agenda." Journal of Psychology and Theology, 23 No. 1 (1995): 16

8. Simão, Talita P.; Caldeira, Sílvia; De Carvalho, Emilia C. 2016. "The Effect of Prayer on Patients' Health: Systematic Literature Review." *Religions* 7, no. 1: 11.

PRAYING FOR OTHERS—THE RESULTS

1. Galton, Francis. "Statistical studies into the efficacy of prayer." *Fortnightly Review,* 12 (1872): 125-135.

2. Joyce, C Richard, and Weldon, RMC. "The Objective Efficacy of Prayer: A double-blind clinical trial." *The Journal of Chronic Diseases*, 18 (1965): 367-377. https://doi.org/10.1016/0021-9681(65)90040-8

3. Collipp, PJ. "The efficacy of prayer: A triple-blind study." *Medical Times*, 97 no. 5 (1969): 201-204.

4. Byrd, Randolph. "Positive therapeutic effects of intercessory prayer in a coronary care unit population." *Southern Medical Journal*, 81 no. 7 (July 1988): 826-829.

5. Byrd, "Positive therapeutic effects," 827.

6. Byrd, "Positive therapeutic effects," 829.

7. Harris, William S, et al. (1999). "A Randomized, Controlled Trial of the Effects of Remote, Intercessory Prayer on Outcomes in Patients Admitted to the Coronary care unit." *Archives of Internal Medicine,* 159 no.19 (1999): 2273-2278. doi:10.1001/archinte.159.19.2273

8. Sicher, F, Targ, E, Moore, D, and Smith, H. (1998). "A randomized, double-blind study of the effect of distant healing in a population with advanced AIDS: Report of a small scale study." *Western Journal of Medicine*, 169 no. 6 (1998): 356-363.

9. Benson, H, Dusek, JA, Sherwood, JB, Lam, P, Bethea, CF, Carpenter, W, Levitsky, S, Hill, PC, Clem DW Jr, Jain, MK,

Dumel, D, Kopecky, SL, Muller PS, Marek, D, Follins, Hibberd, PL. "Study of the therapeutic effects of intercessory prayer (STEP) in cardiac bypass patients – A multi-center randomized trial of uncertainty and certainty of receiving intercessory prayer." *American Heart Journal* 151 no. 4 (April 2006):934-42.

10. Guerin, Scott. "The Effects on Quality of Life on Those who Pray and Meditate for Others." *The International Journal of Healing and Caring.* (Sept 2009) https://www.ijhc.org/the-effects-on-quality-of-life-on-those-who-pray-and-meditate-for-others-scott-guerin

MEDITATION—A COMMON GROUND

1. Benson, Herbert. *Four Decades of Mind Body and Spirituality Findings*. Presented at Spirituality & Healing in Medicine Dec 1-2, 2007 Boston, MA

THE GAME CHANGER—A CONVERSATION WITH GOD

1. Walsch, Neale Donald. *Conversations with God: an uncommon dialogue. Book 1.* New York: G.P. Putnam's Son's, 2002.

2. Walsch, Neale Donald. *The New Revelations: A Conversation with God.* New York: Atria Books, 2002.

3. Walsch, *The New Revelations: A Conversation with God*, 3.

4. Walsch, *The New Revelations: A Conversation with God*, 98.

5. Walsch, *The New Revelations: A Conversation with God*, 9

THE NEXT COURSE—MIRACLES

1. Thetford, William T, and Schucman, Helen. *A Course in Miracles*. Mill Valley, CA: Foundation of Inner Peace, 1975.

2. Thetford and Schucman, *A Course in Miracles*, 8.

3. Thetford and Schucman, *A Course in Miracles*, 10.

4. Thetford and Schucman, *A Course in Miracles,* 11.

5. Thetford and Schucman, *A Course in Miracles,* 25.

A WORD ABOUT AUTOMATIC WRITING

1. Flournoy, Theodore (trans – Daniel B. Vermilye) *From India to the Planet Mars. A study of a case of somnambulism.* Harper & Brothers Publishers, New York. 1901.

2. Albert Einstein Site Online. "Albert Einstein Quotes – Science." Accessed May 15, 2019. http://www.alberteinsteinsite.com/quotes /einsteinquotes.html#religon

3. Kanigel, Robert. *The man who knew infinity: a life of the genius, Ramanujan.* New York: C. Scribner's, 1991.

4. Kanigel, *The man who knew infinity: a life of the genius, Ramanujan,* 281.

5. Kanigel, *The man who knew infinity: a life of the genius, Ramanujan,* 7.

PRAYER 2.0—ATTRACTION

1. Wattles, Wallace D. *The Science of Getting Rich.* Langhorn, Pennsylvania, JonRose Publishing, 1910, p9

2. Wattles, *The Science of Getting Rich,* 17.

3. Wattles, *The Science of Getting Rich,* 65.

4. Hicks, Esther, and Hicks, Jerry. *Ask, and it is Given.* Carlsbad, California, Hay House, Inc. 2004. xxi.

5. Hicks, *Ask, and it is Given,* 25.

HOW THE LAW OF ATTRACTION WORKS

1. Hicks, Esther, and Hicks, Jerry. *Ask, and it is Given.* Carlsbad, California, Hay House, Inc. 2004. 114

2. Byrne, Rhonda. *The Secret*. Atria Books/Beyond Words. 2006. ix

3. Byrne, *The Secret*, 93.

4. Farber, Neil. "The Law of Attraction Revisited." Accessed January 18, 2018. https://www.psychologytoday.com/blog/the-blame-game/201401/the-law-attraction-revisited

5. Farber, Neil. "The Truth about the Law of Attraction." Accessed January 20, 2018. https://www.psychologytoday.com/blog/the-blame-game/201609/the-truth-about-the-law-attraction

6. Dyer, Wayne. "The Power of Intention." Accessed July 20, 2019. https://www.drwaynedyer.com/press/power-intention/

A QUANTUM EXPLANATION

1. Chopra, Deepak, and Kafatos, Menas. *You are the Universe*. New York: Harmony Books. 2017. 148.

2. Roethlisberger, FJ and Dickson, William J. *Volume V Management and the worker*, ed. Kenneth Thompson, London: Routledge, 2003.

3. Battista, John R. "Abraham Maslow, and Roberto Assagioli: Pioneers of Transpersonal Psychology." In *Textbook of Transpersonal Psychiatry and Psychology*, edited by Scotton, Bruce, Chinen, Allen B., Battista, John R, 52-61. New York: BasicBooks, 1996.

4. Wade, Jenny. *Changes of Mind*. Albany: State University of New York Press, 1996.

5. Chopra, Deepak, and Kafatos, Menas. *You are the Universe*, 148.

6. Scharf, Caleb. "This Is What We Don't Know About The Universe." Accessed February 3, 2019. https://blogs.scientificamerican.com/life-unbounded/this-is-what-we-done28099t-know-about-the-universe/

ON BEING ANGELS

1. Dyer, Wayne. *Wisdom of the ages.* Boston: Harper Collins, 2002.

www.ingramcontent.com/pod-product-compliance
Lightning Source LLC
Chambersburg PA
CBHW051352290426
44108CB00015B/1978